DEER ALLIANCE

HUNTER COMPETENCE ASSESSMENT PROGRAMME 2005 - 2010

STALKER TRAINING MANUAL

WRITTEN, COMPILED AND EDITED BY

LIAM M. NOLAN

and

JAMES T. WALSH

FOR THE DEER ALLIANCE
HCAP DEVELOPMENT COMMITTEE, 2004 - 2005

WILD DEER MANAGEMENT IN IRELAND: STALKER TRAINING MANUAL

First published 2005

Second Edition 2008

Nolan, Liam M. & Walsh, James T.

Wild Deer Management in Ireland:
Stalker Training Manual

ISBN 0-9549821-0-X

Printed in Ireland by Standard Printers Ltd., Galway.

Published 2005 by the
Deer Alliance Development Committee
in association with
HCAP Assessment Committee,
P. O. Box 10, Bray, Co. Wicklow, Ireland
Email: HCAP@Ireland.com

HUNTER COMPETENCE ASSESSMENT PROGRAMME 2005 – 2010 STALKER TRAINING MANUAL

INTRODUCTION

Welcome to the Second Edition of the Deer Alliance Stalker Training Manual. Since the Manual was introduced as an aid to preparation for certification under the Hunter Competence Assessment Programme (HCAP) in 2005, it has benefited from an extensive readership and proven invaluable in preparing candidates for assessment. Meanwhile HCAP itself has enjoyed a wide acceptance amongst the deerhunting community and has set a new and better standard for all persons involved in deer management and conservation in Ireland.

HCAP is a collaborative exercise initiated in 2001 and involving some twelve different groups, each having an interest, direct or indirect, in planning for safe, efficient and humane management of wild deer in Ireland. It developed from a requirement imposed by Coillte Teoranta for every licensee or nominated stalker seeking to hunt deer on Coillte forest property, to have achieved a satisfactory level of knowledge and competence, to be measured by an independent authority according to a defined standard.

HCAP was developed to an initial stage of planning and implementation by an alliance of deer interests (the "Deer Alliance") which included the Irish Deer Society, Wild Deer Association of Ireland, Wicklow Deer Management & Conservation Group and Wicklow Deer Society, as well as various independent stalking interests (including commercial stalking interests). Proposals for the HCAP were then further developed by a Development Committee comprised of the above-named deer interests, as well as representatives of Coillte Teoranta, National Parks & Wildlife Service, Forest Service, An Garda Siochana, Irish Farmers' Association and Irish Timber Growers' Association. A Working Committee composed of Liam M. Nolan (Wicklow Deer Group) and James Walsh MRCVS, together with Barry Coad, Deer & Game Manager, Coillte Teoranta and Wesley Atkinson, Deputy Regional Manager, National Parks & Wildlife Service, was appointed in May 2004 to develop the Stalker Training Manual, on which hunter competence assessment is based.

The Stalker Training Manual is intended to reflect and communicate best practice in management and culling of wild deer by licensed hunters operating in Irish conditions. It is also intended to form the basis of educative training courses in stalking and deer management in Ireland, with particular reference to the efficient and humane control of wild deer. Candidates for assessment under HCAP are required to satisfy standards set down and applied by the HCAP Assessment Committee, an independent body established for the purpose and charged with responsibility for monitoring and maintenance of standards in terms of practical and humane control of wild deer.

Candidates are required to satisfactorily complete an examination process and to satisfy assessors in terms of shooting competence and safety awareness under simulated field conditions. Readers should note that the material contained within the Stalker Training Manual is based on best practice guidelines and the highest standards of management of wild deer, including firearms safety, as currently known and recognised. There is no guarantee, implied or otherwise, that assimilation of the material herein, or any subsequent assessment and certification of hunter competence, will necessarily lead to elimination of all possible problems or difficulties associated with stalking and culling of deer in the wild. Any liability arising from error of judgment, carelessness, negligence or from any other reason or cause, on the part of any person hunting wild deer with or without a firearm, whether following study of the Stalker Training Manual, completion of any associated training programme or following certification of competence according to prescribed assessment methodology by the Assessment Committee which will administer the Hunter Competence Assessment Programme, is hereby expressly rejected and denied by the authors and publishers of the Stalker Training Manual, by the Deer Alliance, by all participating bodies and by the HCAP Assessment Committee.

It is hoped that this manual will be of practical use and benefit to all concerned with and interested in wild deer and their conservation and better management, and of relevance and interest to non-hunters as well, imparting as it does an abundance of information on all matters relating to wild deer in Ireland.

Funding and technical support received from Coillte Teoranta, National Parks & Wildlife Service and the Forest Service in support of development of the Stalker Training Manual is gratefully acknowledged. Financial support has also been received from the Irish Deer Society, Wild Deer Association of Ireland, Wicklow Deer Society and Wicklow Deer Management & Conservation Group. The contribution of all concerned with review and where necessary correction of draft material is also gratefully acknowledged, including the input of members of the Development Committee and that of John Melville, Andrew Guthrie and Hazel Sheridan of the Veterinary Section, Department of Agriculture & Food and Mick Healy of Wild Irish Game Ltd. In particular we wish to thank Paul Wood of Screebe Estates, Mark Coombes, John Creedon, Barry Coad, John Griffin and Malcolm Morris BVSc, MRCVS for kindly supplying photographs, without which the end result would not have been possible. Additional photographs were provided by John Robinson, Philip Mugridge, Daniel J. Cox, Jim Walsh and Liam Nolan. New material relating to carcase handling and food safety requirements has been provided for the Second Edition of the Manual by the Food Safety Authority of Ireland, and HCAP-Certified candidates will be treated as Trained Hunters for purposes of interpretation of EU legislation in relation to handling of game.

Finally, full credit must be given to all those participating organisations, bodies and individuals who together provided the impetus and the vehicle for the development and implementation of the Hunter Competence Assessment Programme, whose input made production of the Stalker Training Manual possible and whose continued involvement and support will ensure that the objectives of the programme are fully attained. Specific thanks is given to all those members of the Deer Alliance Development Committee who gave generously of their time and knowledge in support of the Working Committee, including Tim Crowley, Director of Forestry, Coillte Teoranta (Chairman); Liam McGarry, Irish Deer Society; Damian Hannigan, Wild Deer Association of Ireland; John Flynn, Wicklow Deer Society; Noel Spillane, representing independent stalkers; John Fenton, representing commercial stalking interests; Jamie Mulleady, National Parks & Wildlife Service; John Connelly, Forest Service; Det. Sgt. Brian Brunton, An Garda Siochana; Barbara Maguire, Irish Farmers' Association; and Denis Bergin, Irish Timber Growers' Association. Liam Nolan, joint author of the Manual and Secretary of the Deer Alliance HCAP Assessment Committee, was appointed as administrator of the assessment process in 2005 and continues in that capacity.

LIAM M. NOLAN
JAMES T. WALSH MRCVS
BARRY COAD
WESLEY ATKINSON

HUNTER COMPETENCE ASSESSMENT PROGRAMME 2005
STALKER TRAINING MANUAL

CONTENTS

CHAPTER VIII

FIREARMS SAFETY: *Common reasons why accidents occur (in and around vehicles, loading and unloading, negotiating obstacles, crawling or stalking with loaded rifle) - Barrel obstruction - Storage of weapons (recommended security provisions at home and in transport) - Weapon proficiency - Steady shooting positions - Background to shot - Non-firearm risks (knives, weather, dragging) - Health and Safety Agency*

CHAPTER IX

DEER HUNTING AND THE LAW: *Wildlife Act, 1976 – Wildlife (Amendment) Act, 2000 Firearms Acts, 1925 to 2000 – Control of Dogs Act, 1986 – Occupiers' Liability Act, 1995*

CHAPTER X

CARCASE HANDLING: *Bleeding and field evisceration - Carcase examination and disease recognition (veterinary aspects) - Game Meat Directive - Reasons for carcase condemnation - Larder requirements Home Preparation of Venison, Joints etc. - Meat contamination prevention - Food Acts and FSA*

CHAPTER XI

FORESTRY AND DEER: *Overview – Forestry Processes (Planning, Establishment, Maintenance, Inventory, Thinning, Harvesting) – Damaging Impacts from Deer – Reducing/Preventing Damage – Physical Protection – Habitat Management – Deer Control*

CHAPTER XII

IMPACTS OF DEER ON NATURE CONSERVATION HABITATS: *National Heritage Areas Special Areas of Conservation – Special Protection Areas – Grazing, Sporting and Turf-Cutting Rights Conservation Planning*

APPENDICES

CHAPTER I

PRINCIPLES OF DEER MANAGEMENT

Aims and objectives - Current problems facing deer in Ireland - Methods of population assessment - Breeding capacity and size of cull - Planning the Cull - Cull Selection - Shooting Calendar & shooting plan - Record keeping - Public relations

The aim of every deer manager, amateur or professional, should be to maintain deer in a healthy condition, with numbers appropriate to and in balance with local conditions.

This means that he must ensure that deer numbers are kept within levels commensurate with available food supplies and within whatever levels of tolerance are accorded locally, having regard for landowner interests, in particular forestry, given that a majority of stalkers will find their shooting focussed on land owned by Coillte Teoranta and managed by them for timber production. Damage to surrounding agricultural land and farm crops will also be a useful indicator of local deer populations. The farming and farm forestry sectors are acutely aware of increasing levels of damage from deer. The stalker must be aware of signs of measurable damage to forestry or agricultural interests and he must be prepared to cull deer carefully and systematically when called upon to do so. In doing this he must operate within an environment which is not always directly controlled by him and which conforms to objectives set down by others.

In recent years, a range of factors has led to a substantial increase in the wild deer population, locally and nationally. These factors are examined elsewhere in this manual but meanwhile have necessarily led to a review of practices, procedures and objectives in deer management, especially on lands owned or managed by Coillte Teoranta. This, coupled with a corresponding increase in the number of non-professional deer hunters now applying for an annual licence to hunt wild deer, has in turn led to a recognition for a greater knowledge and understanding of principles of wild deer management amongst even occasional deerstalkers. Considerations of efficiency as well as of safety also demand highest standards of best practice. In summary, it is recognised as incumbent on the non-professional deer hunter that the requirements for knowledge are no less for him than they are for the person engaged professionally.

The density of deer acceptable locally must be decided upon and decisions taken also as to how to balance the need for objective cull criteria with the simpler sporting activity of deer hunting. A procedure must be set up to set a cull and assess its success or failure.

Effective deer management is founded on the following essential choices:

1: Reduce damage to trees and agricultural crops. This is impossible to prevent but can be kept to a minimum with an acceptable harvest of deer.

2: Keep the deer population healthy and in balance with the food available. This can be achieved by either:

(a) Artificially feeding the deer. Seldom practical and with inherent disease risks.

(b) Reduce the deer population to such a low level that interference with normal forest operations is minimal or non-existent. Again, rarely practical or possible, particularly in thick conifer woodland, also questionable ethically on the ground of woodland biodiversity.

(c) Increase the natural food available, by leaving unplanted 'deer glades' and stream edges, at the same time reducing the deer population to a point where naturally growing food is sufficient to avoid serious crop damage. Although this option at first sight appears to reduce the area of productive land available for agricultural or forestry use, it may reduce crop damage to an acceptable level.

3: Balance the losses due to deer damage against the benefits which they may bring in terms of amenity value, both from being viewed by the public, the rent accrued from stalking leases and in the case of some private estates, the income from venison sold. In fairness to deer, in relation to forestry damage, a distinction must be drawn between damage caused by deer and that caused by sheep and both the deer manager and the forester must learn to recognise the difference. It is still custom and practice in many places for sheep farmers to let their flocks graze freely in forestry, with or without formal permission or right.

Where deer numbers must be controlled, the only practical way of doing it is with a rifle. The stalker must be safe, knowledgeable and competent. The basis of this manual is to educate the stalker to the level where he can assess and manage a deer population properly and humanely, understanding the responsibilities that go with it. However there is no substitute for experience. The novice stalker should make it his business to go out with those who are more experienced and learn at first hand, by observation and shared experience, the potential for damage by deer and how to deal with it. He should talk with the landowner or forester to discover where the deer are feeding, learn their movement patterns and the possible numbers involved and gain some insight into age and gender breakdown.

It is the number of adult females in a population that governs the rate of increase of a population. The following example shows the rate of increase of a herd of twenty adult females over a five-year period if no management is applied. It assumes a 90% calf survival to one year and a 50:50 sex ratio at birth.

	Adult Females	Adult Males	Yearlings	Juveniles	Total Population
Spring Year 1	20	-	-	-	20
Autumn Year 1	20	-	-	18	38
Autumn Year 2	20	-	18	18	56
Autumn Year 3	29	9	18	26	82
Autumn Year 4	38	18	26	34	116
Autumn Year 5	51	31	34	45	161

If the basic concept of management is to control the number of deer in an area to the carrying capacity of the ground, then there are a number of factors which need to be considered. These include assessment of the number of deer involved and the level of damage sustained in the given area of land.

Wild goats can also cause damage in forestry plantations. Feral goats are not a protected species under the Wildlife Act, 1976 (as amended)

Planning the cull

A great many stalkers, if not a majority, will hunt their quarry on Coillte forest property, in which case they will be attempting to achieve the designated cull for the forest area in question. The designated cull is based on local observations and estimates of deer population, and the amount of actual or potential damage from deer. It is simply stated as X number of male deer and Y number of female deer. This cull is the licensee's primary target and to some extent, continued access to deer hunting depends on achieving it.

In other situations, the stalker may also be a manager and have the opportunity of planning the annual cull with an eye to varying objectives.

For many years, management planning has elsewhere been based on alternative theories, depending on factors such as nature of terrain, deer species, levels of damage and local objectives as to maintenance, reduction or increase of deer numbers, or trophy quality.

One such theory is based on the Hoffman Pyramid, much written about but complex to understand and difficult to implement – and almost impossible to employ under conditions of heavy woodland. Nonetheless it remains a useful starting point and all stalkers should familiarise themselves with the underlying theory. To this end, a detailed explanation is set out as an appendix to this manual.

In Ireland, environmental considerations demand a more immediate approach, especially in the context of a rapidly expanding population of deer and the serious potential for damage as populations expand exponentially.

Focus must therefore be on culling of female deer, as discussed in detail in this chapter. Where numbers are a measurable problem, females of any age should be culled. After that, juveniles of either sex should be the target. Mature males are next on the list – bearing in mind that the number of adult male deer culled has very little impact on the overall population. Consideration should be given to allowing adolescent males to mature and thus offer some trophy potential. Cull planning starts with population assessment.

Methods of population assessment

Unfortunately, it is next to impossible to accurately assess the number of deer in a given population. It is of course easier in an open mountain situation, but deer move in and out of a given area depending on the time of year and on disturbance. Time spent in reconnaissance is never time wasted – indeed, it is absolutely essential for efficient deer management. It is vital to know what deer are on the ground, including details of species, age and gender, for only when you know how many deer you have can you plan the cull and so guard against future damage. In many situations deer are missed and not counted and in some, there are cases of double counting. A good initial guide is to assess for evidence of deer damage to trees growing in the area. This is a good indication as to whether the deer density is too high, though the farmer or forester may already have told you this. Identification of deer damage is discussed elsewhere in this manual but it must be distinguished from that caused by rabbits, hares, sheep and goats. COFORD (National Council for Forest Research & Development) have also identified grey squirrels as a significant pest species in woodland.

There are a number of different methods of assessing the population in a given area. All will give a guideline but seldom an accurate reading. For the purposes of deer management, an estimate is sufficient. A truly accurate count is virtually impossible, but the trend as to whether the population is increasing or decreasing is important. It is important that each count is conducted at the same time of year so that numbers can be compared and population trends can be deduced.

Learn to differentiate between damage caused by hares, sheep, goats and deer. Hares are protected under the Wildlife Act, 1976 (as amended) and (excluding certain townlands in Co. Wexford) may be hunted from the 26th day of September in any year to the 28th day of February in the following year, both dates inclusive. No licence is required other than the licence associated with an Open or Unlimited firearm certificate for a shotgun. They may not be shot with a rifled firearm.

Where possible, the assessment should be done by the same team of people each year. As well as giving a reasonable idea of deer numbers, visual deer counts can also provide a sex breakdown and an assessment of age and general body condition of the herd. If the area being counted is of sufficient size and any movement of deer in and out of the area is consequently at a minimal level, then it can be a useful tool to help adjust the cull level for the following year.

Grey squirrel

Red squirrel

The grey squirrel is now an established pest species in Irish woodland. It is not a protected species under the Wildlife Act, 1976 (as amended). Note however that red squirrels are fully protected at all times in Ireland under the Wildlife Act, 1976 (as amended)

Open ground counts

Open ground counts are only suitable for red and sika deer on the open mountain. March is the best time of year for visual deer counts At this time of year, it is still easy to distinguish between hinds and calves, the stags still retain their antlers and vegetation levels are at their lowest.

The best way to conduct an open ground count is for a sufficient number of people to line up abreast across a hill and move in a prearranged direction. It is important to minimize the amount of dead ground that could hide deer. The counting team members should chart the number and sex of the deer they saw, where they were, time seen and the direction in which the deer moved. These notes and maps are then compared at the end of the day to eliminate double counting and a population assessment is arrived at.

While once-a-year counts are probably sufficient, in areas of open ground a more accurate result might be obtained with a subsequent count about a month after calving, and combining the results of both surveys.

Woodland counts

Estimating deer in woodland is quite a different proposition. Visibility is obviously a problem, especially in thick conifer woodland. In these cases pellet group counts are probably the best option to assess deer density. However as the feeding in conifer forestry is often poor, the animals using it usually leave the wood to feed at night and a good estimate can be achieved by lamping surrounding fields at night. This requires a licence from National Parks & Wildlife Service.

Remember that deer have a preference for young forestry, where they can graze between the trees. As the trees grow and light becomes shade, the vegetation beneath then dies off. It then increases again as trees are thinned and the canopy is broken. The feeding value decreases and the deer generally move to a different area or section of the plantation. It then increases again as trees are thinned and the canopy opens. Care must be taken not to assume that the density of deer will be the same in different age class blocks.

One method of counting deer that can be used in suitable woodland blocks is to move deer slowly so that they cross a ride line or road on which a number of people are positioned, another team of people walk slowly, preferably with steady dogs and push the deer towards those counting. The beaters should move slowly and quietly, gently tapping trees with a stick. This will not work in thicket-stage conifers where most deer tend to lie up and wait for the line to pass.

Sika prickets are easily counted in the late summer and early autumn

Vantage point observation

This is a relatively effective method where the topography of a forest allows. It involves watching an area of woodland edge and possibly a few forest clearings from an elevated point for a few hours, with binoculars, at dawn and at dusk - periods of peak deer activity. Deer are assessed in groups as they move and graze. Make-up of these groups is important as it means that they can be discounted from another observer's total should they move into his view. These counts should be repeated a number of times over a few days and the highest count taken as the estimated population for the observed area. Should say, one-fifth of a block of forestry be counted in such a way, the total count can be extrapolated as five times the count as the total for the whole forest only if the counted area is a good average of the age and species class for the whole block.

Tracks and slots

A stalker can gain a good idea of the number of deer on his ground by simply looking at the tracks left in wet or boggy areas. While not a strict count, the tracks seen on banks and crossing points of ditches will give some idea of density. Familiarize yourself with the difference between deer and sheep footprints. Try to visit your ground after a fall of snow, when a good assessment of deer numbers can often be obtained from looking at the number of deer tracks.

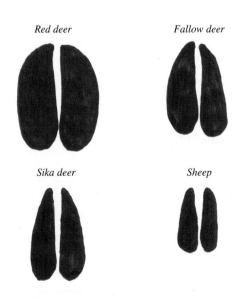

Red deer *Fallow deer*

Sika deer *Sheep*

Pellet group counts

Pellet group counts involves the counting of piles of deer faecal pellets in a strict fashion in plots along a transect line. Obviously the presence or abundance of deer pellet groups will be related to the density of the deer. There is a variation in the rate of decay of faeces dependant on the site involved. In wet or high rainfall areas pellets will break down faster than on sheltered ground. Although the methodology of this form of population assessment is too detailed for the scope of this manual it may be the only reasonably reliable method capable of being used in large thick forestry plantations.

Fresh deer scat

When counting pellet groups, learn to tell the difference between sheep, rabbit and deer droppings

Cohort analysis

Probably one of the most accurate methods of measuring deer numbers, cohort analysis is retrospective and extremely time consuming. It involves aging all deer shot and working back to their date of birth. For example – take a hypothetical situation where, in a ten-year window all the stalkers have shot forty deer in a particular forest, all of which can be traced back, by jaw aging, to having been born in one particular year. Assuming 80% calf survival (remembering that calf survival rate will depend on species, weather conditions, food supply and general habitat, amongst other considerations), then there had to have been a minimum of fifty hinds on the ground in that year.

A cruder method of analysing the cohort is by assessing prickets. In the early part of the season, sika prickets in particular are quite easily seen and differentiated from one another by their antler shapes. Should you see or shoot ten different prickets, assuming for each one of them there is a female yearling, that makes twenty calves, and using the previous example therefore, there would have been a minimum of twenty-five hinds the previous year. Remember to make allowance in your calculations for any females culled after calving the previous year.

To be effective, deer fencing must be at least two metres high

All the above methods are time consuming and therefore costly when man-hour cost is a factor. It is important to understand the basis of assessing deer density but in reality the results will not be very accurate. At some stage the stalker or landowner will have to estimate a number for a particular area, having regard for habitat type and age class of the trees, and set a cull accordingly. From this regular assessment of indicators of deer damage, allow for adjustment in succeeding years.

A high deer density in a particular area may not be a problem if further assessment shows low levels of deer damage. However in another area, with different conditions, a much lower density of deer could be doing a higher level of damage. The deer stalker must understand that in such areas it is quite justifiable to shoot heavily to allow establishment of a young crop, while in later years the planting will be less susceptible to damage.

In many parts of the country it has now become essential to protect broadleaf plantings with two metre high deer fencing or with individual tree guards, because deer are causing unacceptable levels of damage. This has huge cost implications on the viability of forestry as an alternative farming enterprise. Even in native broadleaf plantations, natural regeneration is being hampered by the presence of excessive numbers of deer.

Alder tree with individual tree shelter

Assessment of age profile and reproductive capacity can be obtained by the stalker by examining jaws and ovaries/uteri of culled deer. For the deer species found in Ireland, where the possibility of twins is negligible, and assuming an equal number of males and females in that population, the cull should be approximately 25% of the spring census (equal numbers of males and females). In reality, there is likely to be a sex imbalance with more females than males in the population so perhaps a more realistic figure, particularly for sika deer, would be 30-33% of the Spring count. However if an under-estimate has been made in the census or if damage is worse than expected, the cull should be increased, with emphasis placed on removing more females. Shooting any number of male deer will have no effect on the rate of increase of a deer population.

Record Keeping

Accurate record-keeping is essential for effective deer management. Cull targets are based on estimates generated in the field but may not always be accurate, having regard for itinerant deer and fluctuations in resident herd numbers. All stalkers should carefully record all deer seen in the course of field outings, together with a detailed record of all deer shot. Records should include:

- Date
- Time of day
- Weather conditions
- Number of deer seen, broken down by species, age and gender
- Note any and all special circumstances e.g. any special characteristics or behaviour of deer seen
- Number of deer shot including details of species, age and gender and any and all special features or characteristics (and especially including any factors impacting on health of deer shot)

The number of deer seen, as well as the number culled, will provide the basis for the ongoing management plan for the area and will remove elements of guesswork. Coillte Teoranta require a detailed cull return as a term and condition of the annual deer stalking licence. Renewal of the annual deer hunting licence by National Parks & Wildlife Service also requires a return of deer shot, including details of where shot, species and sex.

Specific problems associated with deer management

Habitat

Attaining the cull is the essential prerequisite of any deer management plan. In Ireland this problem has historically been exacerbated by extensive blocks of thick coniferous woodland, planted with little thought to the eventual culling of the deer population. In many of these forests deer can live in a small area, never really moving to a place where they can be culled. The size of red deer in particular can sometimes make carcase extraction near impossible in some areas of extensive forestry which have poor access.

Browsing damage can occur even in deer glades

Thankfully, a little more thought has been put into forest planning in recent years but unfortunately it takes time for plantations to mature and to be replanted with deer management in mind. Areas of the forest should be left unplanted to form deer lawns – open glades where deer can graze and where the deer manager can see the deer, whether to count, to assess or to cull. The banks of rivers and streams provide good grazing and the gentle curves on the edge of forestry often constitute productive areas for stalking. Areas of hardwoods should be planted or at least include sections of larch, a deciduous conifer, to give relatively open areas during the culling season. Rides should be left wide enough in conifer woodland for light to get in and to allow grasses to grow. This not only provides feeding for deer and reduces tree damage, it also provides good open areas for shooting.

Disturbance of deer

The great mistake when stalking deer is to continually put them under stress through disturbance over the entire culling season. This has a couple of negative aspects to it; firstly, it makes it much more difficult to achieve the cull and secondly, the added stress keeps the deer inside the woodland for longer periods of time, often only emerging well after dark. Both or either of these factors may increase the damage levels within the forestry block.

Unfortunately, the rising cost of many Coillte deer hunting licences (and indeed, licences to hunt wild deer on other privately-owned land) has meant that many primary licence holders or sporting rights leaseholders have to take in additional stalkers to meet the financial outlay and the ground is hunted three or four times weekly. Fallow deer in particular will often move out of such an area altogether until the season is over. Deer become alert and jumpy and it becomes impossible to meet the cull. Stalkers should be aware of their responsibility to meet the designated cull and if necessary, limit stalking activity to short periods of high intensity, with a number of rifles placed in prearranged places at the same time. The forest should then be given a few weeks rest in between if at all possible. High seat shooting, to be discussed later, greatly reduces disturbance.

Shooting from high seats minimises disturbance on the stalking ground

Shooting from vehicles is both illegal and counterproductive. While initially a number of naive deer can be accounted for, they very soon associate the sound of a vehicle with danger. A fear of vehicles then makes it difficult to assess the number of deer in a forest come the end of the season.

Insufficient cull of female deer

For many years there has been a substantial imbalance between the number of male and female deer shot. This is due to a number of factors, not least that historically the male deer season ran for six months while the female season was only three months in length, with the exception of Dublin and Wicklow where the season ran for four months. Recent changes in seasons are designed to help to address this imbalance.

It is regrettable that many stalkers do not take their hind cull seriously. They assume that shooting any deer will lead to a reduction in the local deer population. Many of these deer shooters are also involved in game shooting and with the onset of the hind and doe season coinciding with the opening of the pheasant season, their attention is drawn elsewhere. This situation is not helped by inclement weather during the latter half of the season. On some private estates where pheasant shooting is a commercial business, the amount of woodland disturbance from November to January makes the female cull very difficult even where the stalker puts in all the time needed.

One of the main reasons why the culling of female deer is more difficult than that of male deer is that from November onwards the days are shorter and deer can feed all night undisturbed. Deer at this time of year do not have large demands on energy (a natural phenomenon in deer known as winter inappetence). However, towards the middle of February the foetus in the hind is getting larger, demand for food becomes greater and the days become longer. At this time of the year female deer spend more time grazing and become increasingly available for culling at dawn and dusk (subject to Open and Closed Season dates).

When a hind and calf are encountered together, especially early in the season, shoot the calf first

The stalker as deer manager should try to shoot as many females as possible in early November, as they become a good deal less visible from December. It also helps to reduce pressure on the grass and bramble available for feeding over the winter months – in itself reducing the damage to the tree crop. Preference at this time of year should be given to shooting calves and yearling hinds. When a hind and calf are found together, always shoot the calf first. If you must shoot an accompanied female first, it is often possible to take the calf by remaining concealed for a period of time. This can occasionally work in reverse. If a calf doesn't return to the area of its mother's carcase within a reasonable time, it may or may not be old enough to live independently – although evidence does suggest that survival rates of early-orphaned calves (whose dams have been culled early in the season) are very poor. The better practice is to always shoot the calf first.

When attempting the female cull every opportunity must be taken to attain the required number. While not recommended for the novice stalker, a neck shot will drop a deer with less disturbance to a group than a chest shot, which causes the deer to rush forward.

Correct shot placement is discussed in detail later. Sound moderators are also useful where multiple animals are required to be removed, and have become increasingly popular in recent years.

.243 rifle fitted with bipod and sound moderator

Close-up of sound moderator on .243 calibre barrel

Natural movement of deer

The biology of deer and the individual characteristics of each species will be discussed later. The stalker must understand that there is a change in behaviour of deer at different times of the year and that this will effect the census and cull plan on any given forest or estate. The deer species found in Ireland are non-territorial in nature. Mature males and females live apart for most of the year.

Farmers often experience heavy grazing on spring grass from deer in March and April. The season is closed and ordinarily, it is unlikely that a licence will be issued to shoot them out of season unless damage is severe. Deer are likely to be drawn to the area only because of the lack of feeding elsewhere and they may not be seen in the same area in the autumn. These are the worst months of the year for feed availability. Well-fertilized spring grass, particularly near forests or heather uplands, is likely to draw in large numbers of deer at this time of year, but within a short period they will usually have dispersed. Nonetheless, it may be necessary from time to time, in specific circumstances, to cull deer out of season under a "Section 42" licence, where unacceptable levels of damage, including grazing on grassland, is experienced.

Deer can cause crop damage in any area in the summer months. Often there are very few female deer in the area and most of the animals involved are stags. As soon as September comes and the season opens, the stags disperse. It can then be difficult to shoot the target number and the problem recurs the following year.

Sheep fencing can occasionally lead to loss of deer, which may become entangled in wire and subsequently die

Water proves no obstacle to the movement of deer where they are motivated to enter or cross it

These are some of the practical problems associated with deer management. In some cases it is possible to get a licence to shoot deer out of season or with a lamp at night. These licences, known as "Section 42 licences", are issued by the National Parks & Wildlife Service, but only on a case-by-case examination by a local Conservation Ranger. As a matter of policy, where out-of-season control becomes necessary on Coillte forest property, Coillte will themselves take the appropriate action; Coillte sporting licences allow the licencee and any nominated stalkers to hunt deer only during the designated open season.

Fallow deer management

Proper management of a fallow deer population has different problems than those associated with red and sika deer, where dense plantations are the biggest obstacle to control. Lowland fallow deer habitat is often overgrown with bracken and bramble and fallow range over a much wider area. A small block of woodland may be devoid of deer when visited by the stalker but be home to a herd of twenty or more transient deer a week later. Stalkers must be aware that they will in all probability share the herd with a number of other stalking groups in the vicinity and a cooperative stance should be decided upon when it comes to the management of numbers.

Fallow bucks are often over-exploited, prickets and two-year-old bucks being relatively easy to shoot during the rut. Few fallow bucks make it through to maturity, by which time they have learned to live an almost nocturnal existence during the open season. Males are also vulnerable because they tend to travel over a wide area in the course of the year.

Fallow are extremely sensitive to disturbance and will leave an area if disturbance is excessive. This relates not just to stalking but to bird shooting, trail-bike riding and also some forestry operations. They quickly learn the usual stalking routes in a forest, particularly if used regularly every weekend, as is often the case. In problem areas, a number of stalkers operating together in a controlled way can be productive as it tends to get fallow deer up, slowly moving and visible. High seats are particularly useful for the management of fallow deer.

Fallow deer can cause significant damage in agricultural crops

Fallow deer in woodland

Public Relations

In the case of Coillte forest licences, shared forest usage is a feature of the annual shooting plan and this is recognised within the limitations of the Coillte licence e.g. hours of access and during which deer may be shot, whether or not mid-week stalking is permitted or any special requirement associated with public use of forest areas. The restriction on shooting along or across forest rides is another example.

In this context it behoves the deerstalker to practise sensible public relations at all times. Remember, you are in the forest as a licensee, not by right, and you must avoid all occasions of confrontation with a public which may be less than aware of the value of the function you are performing as someone entrusted with achievement of the necessary cull. The same principles apply if shooting on privately owned farmland, with the added onus of ensuring best possible relations with the landowner and any members of the public whom he may ordinarily allow to access his land, for whatever purpose. You may be doing the farmer a service but he is providing you with a sporting resource, which is to be protected. Make yourself aware of "The Country Code" as outlined in the appendix to this manual and practise it always.

None of this is to suggest that you need to be at all defensive about your role in deer management. The fact is that (as previously stated) culling by shooting is the only practical way to control deer numbers, to the benefit of both deer and human economic interests. Your role is to control deer numbers and to cull surplus animals, especially old or infirm animals or those for which the available food supply is insufficient. In so doing you are contributing to the health and overall conservation of the local deer population and for this, you need never apologise.

Nonetheless it is important to be aware of a level of public ignorance of the mechanics of population control and conservation through passive preservation may be the over-riding thought of a member of the public who happens to stumble on the end result of the cull exercise. If necessary, be prepared to give a simple explanation of what is involved, having first established your bona fides and legal entitlement to do what you are doing. Avoid confrontation or rudeness or any insensitive attitude towards public feelings. If in doubt, or if faced with aggressive behaviour, do not respond with aggression or rudeness. Follow best-practice guidelines at all times.

CHAPTER II

BASIC DEER BIOLOGY

*Pregnancy duration and demands. - Antler development, calcification and casting -
Hormonal changes leading to rut – Predators - Recognition of poor calves -
Recognition of adults in poor condition, sick or ailing - Normal life spans and diet
affecting tooth wear - Coat changes*

Deer are classified into the Cervidae family, which is further divided into five sub families. It is the subfamily cervinae that are of interest to us in Ireland, with all our three species included. These are the red deer (Cervus elaphus) and the Japanese sika deer (Cervus Nippon), which are closely related and can hybridise, and the fallow deer (Dama dama). The individual characteristics of these species will be dealt with in further chapters.

Deer are ruminants. All herbivores or grass eaters have adapted to eat plant food which, because it contains cellulose, is poorly digestible. This poor quality food has to be broken down in the gut. Ruminants have developed a four-chambered stomach consisting of the rumen, reticulum, omasum and abomasum. The plant material is ingested and mixed with bacteria and digestion begins. It is later regurgitated in a process known as chewing the cud, when the food is further broken down before being swallowed again and further digestion of cellulose continues. The chewing is done by the back molar teeth, which gradually wear down with time. The degree of wear is dependant very much on the fibre content of the food; animals on a good quality lower fibre diet tend to have slower tooth wear and therefore in general live longer. The constant wearing down of teeth enables the stalker to age an animal by tooth wear. This process will be discussed in more detail later. Deer are prey animals and the presence of such a digestive system allows them to graze continuously while feeding until the rumen is full. This can be done at night or at dawn or dusk, when the risk from predators is at a minimum. When they are finished feeding they can then return to cover to ruminate in relative safety. Natural habitat is the woodland edge though in some areas, such as Kerry and Wicklow, deer have adapted to the open mountain. The difference in the plane of nutrition between upland and woodland areas gives rise to considerable changes in body size and antler development, particularly in the red deer of the Killarney area.

*Deer are ruminants, having a digestive system adapted for
the efficient digestion of plant material*

Deer have very acute senses, as many a deer hunter has found to his cost. The senses of hearing and scent are particularly important. Large ears high on the head allow deer to pick up small sounds over a long distance. Deer have the ability to move each ear independently to pinpoint the source of the sound, allowing the head to remain still so as not to give away the deer's own position.

Large ears, high on the head, give deer an acute sense of hearing

The sense of smell is not only vital to protect against predators but also as a means of communication between deer of the same species.

A suspicious but still curious sika hind tests the wind

Deer possess suborbital (under the eye), interdigital (between the toes) and metatarsal (below the hock joint) scent glands. The suborbital glands are used to mark out territory, particularly by males during the rut. The interdigital glands leave scent marks on the ground and amongst other things, help deer to regroup when scattering after being alarmed.

The animal's sense of sight is not as good as many think. Deer have difficulty making out objects at any but the shortest distance, but their sight is well adapted to picking up movement. This explains the fact that often someone watching a deer will be 'stared down' for a long while by a deer as it tries to make out what it is that caused the movement that it spotted. Assuming the wind is in the stalker's face and the stalker stays quiet, he can often be in full view of a wild deer and remain undetected - as long as he remain absolutely still.

Wild deer in Ireland have no animal predators other than man, and occasionally, dogs. Foxes can of course take newborn calves.

Adult foxes will occasionally kill weak or vulnerable calves

Male Deer

The annual cycle of the male deer is governed by testosterone secretion from the testicles. The most distinguishing feature of male deer is their antlers. In the deer species found in Ireland, only males carry antlers. The growth, casting and re-growth of such headgear are entirely due to changes in these hormones over the year.

*Young sika stag immediately
after casting of antlers*

*Young male deer develop their antlers from pedicles
on either side of the skull*

Young male deer develop pedicles just below the skin on each side of the skull. These pedicles become the foundations on which the antlers will grow in later years. They are narrow in diameter at first and with each year they widen and get slightly lower. The size and shape of the pedicle can therefore give the deerstalker an idea of the age of the stag that he is looking at. The first set of antlers starts to develop in the male deer's first spring. They are initially small hairy bumps, which gradually grow over the months.

Male deer must feed hard over the spring and summer. They will have lost a good deal of body condition in the rut the previous autumn and there will have been little food available during the winter. They now have to grow a whole new set of antlers and put on sufficient muscle and body fat reserves to carry them through the next autumn/winter cycle.

Towards autumn, as the days become shorter, the testicles start to swell and produce more of the male hormone testosterone. As this builds up the growing antlers start to calcify i.e. the soft spongy antler tissue starts to harden and become bone. While growing, the antler is covered with "velvet", a highly active blood-filled tissue which feeds the growing antler.

The velvet feeds the growing antler as it calcifies

Damage to the body of the antler while growing can grossly distort the antler growth for that year, however the antler will in most cases grow normally the following year. However damage to the pedicle at the base of the antler will give rise to permanent damage to subsequent antlers. As growth of the antler nears completion, the base swells and a coronet forms. Progressive narrowing of the blood vessels causes the velvet skin to die and it peels off the antler, which is now dry white bone.

The growth of a new set of antlers places significant demands on the body's energy reserves

The antlers of this hybrid stag were damaged in velvet. Although calcified in that year, they would have grown normally the following year

The deer tries to rid itself of this dangling velvet by rubbing it on trees and bushes; at this stage all pain receptors in the antler are dead. In general it is the bigger males that come into hard antler first. The colour and type of soil and vegetation in the animal's habitat give rise to the colouration of the antlers. Particularly dark-coloured antlers are found in conifer forests on peaty soil where the combination of the resin from spruce trees and the dark colour of the soil combine to give an almost black colouration to the antlers. The tips are usually worn smooth so very little stain adheres to these areas and they therefore appear white.

Antlers are essential to mature stags and bucks in the breeding season. They mark their territory at rutting stands by thrashing the branches of young trees. This is particularly true of fallow deer. Deer also use their antlers for fighting, though conflict usually only arises between males of similar size. In general smaller animals will steer away from animals with larger headgear. Antler size, though the product of genetics and in some cases hybridization, in terms of general quality reflects age and feeding, so that those animals with a big set of antlers are also those that tend to have a heavy body weight. Body size and size of antlers are generally of equal importance when it comes to dominance within the group.

Shedding of velvet causes no discomfort to stags

The aggression towards other males in the rut is another consequence of the high levels of circulating blood testosterone. Rutting activity starts to wane as a result of exhaustion as during this period male deer feed only intermittently if at all and spend most of their time keeping other males away from their rutting stand or group of females depending on the species involved.

The gradual turn of the year, signalled by the shortest day in late December, brings with it a message to the testicles to stop producing testosterone. The secondary sexual characteristics evident in males at this time of year - thickened necks and manes in red and sika deer and the prominent Adam's apple in fallow deer - all start to recede. The aggression between individual male deer reduces and groups of male deer, so evident during the summer months, start to form again.

Damage to the growing antler, in this case a sika stag entangled in netting, can cause extreme pain, as evidenced by trauma to the affected antler

Male deer become vocal during the rut. Fallow bucks groan, red stags roar and sika stags whistle. The amount of vocalization is in direct relation to the level of competition for females. In the Wicklow area, sika stags can be heard whistling from mid August through to the end of December, though no one stag would do it for this long. In general the more mature animals start the rut and as they become exhausted then the younger animals start. Late season rutting is usually as a result of a hind possibly miscarrying a pregnancy and coming into a second heat late in the season; or possibly a late female calf coming into heat for the first time.

As the hormone levels drop, antler casting occurs. This is due to the breaking of the bond between the coronet of the antler and the pedicle of the skull. The two antlers normally shed within a very short period of each other. The exposed pedicle bleeds for the day and then heals over and within a couple of days the new growth of velvet starts.

Vocalisation is important during the rut. Note the heavy mane on this roaring red stag

Antler shape is specific for each of the three species of deer found in Ireland and they will be discussed further in the relevant chapters, but all species produce single-pointed antlers in the first year. These animals are known by a variety of terms, including prickets, spikers and knobbers. They then increase in size and shape depending on feed availability, up to a maximum around 8 to 10 years of age, after which there is an obvious decline in quality year on year. These older heads are described as 'going back'.

Occasionally some male deer, particularly red deer, fail to produce antlers. Known as hummels, they are normal in every other way, often being much bigger in body size as they do not expend energy in producing a new set of antlers every summer.

Some stags get injuries to the testicles while fighting during the rut. These injuries can effectively castrate the animal. The sudden drop in circulating testosterone will cause the stag to shed its antlers irrespective of the time of year, and a new set will start to grow. However because there is then no stimulus for the antlers to calcify the antlers remain in velvet all year round.

Antler quality deteriorates with age, as evidenced by the head of this aged fallow buck

Red and sika hinds and fallow does will eat the placenta soon after calving

Female Deer

The doe or hind will drop its young in the early part of the summer, dependant on species. This is usually done in a regular nursery area, often near to the spot where the dam was herself born.

In herding species, particularly on the open hill, the female will move away from other deer in the group to give birth. She will eat the placenta or afterbirth after delivering the calf. This provides her with extra nutrition but also removes the smell of blood which would attract foxes to the general area. After an hour the young deer will have been licked dry and can usually stand and suckle. As soon as it can walk, it is led away to a nearby spot where it hides up in long grass or bracken.

The young deer gives off little scent at this stage. It will remain completely motionless when approached by any other animal. It will not defecate on its own and so avoids generating any other odour. The stimulus to defecate is provided by the hind licking the anal area; she licks away the faeces as it is passed, so keeping the scent levels down.

Young deer, like this hybrid calf, will remain motionless if approached

While the mother does not normally graze immediately in the vicinity of the bedded youngster, she is never far away, Often a walker who unwittingly passes close by to the concealed calf will be accosted by the hind running in and grunting. The female deer only has contact with her young three or four times in any twenty-four-hour period in order to suckle and groom it.

Sometimes young deer of this age are picked up by well-meaning people who assume that they have been abandoned. This is seldom if ever the case and if picked up or handled, they should be returned to where they are found as soon as possible.

Within a week or two the young deer is spending much of its time with the mother. Very often, at this age, a number of young deer will bed down together in nursery groups. The dam continues suckling the calf until November/December, depending on its age and the level of feeding available. For this reason it is important, when culling deer early in the female open season, that preference always be given to culling the juvenile deer first.

The hind has to reach a critical weight before she will come into heat, so a late female calf of the previous year will be unlikely to reach that weight by the time of the rut. At a time when winter feeding is scarce, either due to severe weather conditions or too high a deer density, a lactating hind may lose too much condition and not have sufficient time to regain it over the summer months. She will then not come into season. This allows her to escape a pregnancy and regain condition in time for the following autumn. This is a particular feature of open ground red deer. Such an animal is known as a yeld hind.

The calves will remain with their mothers until long after they are weaned, learning from them the geography of the area, feeding places and recognition of the various threats that they are likely to encounter in the future. The female calves or fawns will remain as part of the home group, but the males in the second year will be pushed out of the group. These wandering yearling males can travel long distances before linking up with a bachelor group.

Under Irish conditions nearly every female deer of breeding age produces a calf. Given generally good weather conditions, an absence of any predators other than foxes and, as we shall see in a later chapter, very few disease problems, there is substantial potential for rapid growth in deer numbers. It is deer management, the basis of this manual, which allows us to keep the population in check.

Sika hind and calf in mid summer

CHAPTER III

RED DEER

Identification and Distribution - History in Ireland
- Particulars of the rut - Kerry red deer

Red deer are Ireland's largest land mammal. Once widespread, changes in habitat, in particular in the 17th century, and excessive hunting around the time of the famine in the nineteenth century led to a substantial reduction in numbers and distribution. Red deer are related to wapiti, the North American elk and the various species of Asiatic sika deer. Irish red deer were the most westerly race in the grouping Cervus elaphus atlanticus which also included Scottish and Norwegian red deer but each population had its own characteristics. Many of the park deer that were introduced to Ireland contain genes from Eastern European red deer, and also probably some wapiti and sika blood. There are several distinct populations of red deer in Ireland each with its own history, which are discussed below.

Co. Kerry

The remnant herd of what is considered to be the last of the "native" Irish red deer is to be found in the Killarney area of Co. Kerry. The main stronghold is in the mountains to the west and south of Lough Leane, having been given protection at the time by the Muckross and Kenmare estates. The herd is not completely pure in that there were a number of introductions of stags to improve antler quality in the 19th century. The significance of this population and its close proximity with sika deer, and the fact that there is to date no evidence of hybridization between the two species, has led to special protection being accorded to this herd. No red deer can be hunted in Co. Kerry. Hunting, particularly during the rut, can break up established breeding herds and increase the chance of mating between red and sika deer.

While red deer have spread over a large area in Co. Kerry and into Co. Cork, the majority are to be found within the Killarney National Park. The population has increased from just 110 animals in 1970 to about 1,000 today.

Red deer stag in Killarney National Park. Red deer are especially protected in Co. Kerry and may not be shot

Red deer hinds in woodland, Co. Donegal

Co. Donegal

This population, though originating in Co. Donegal, now extends across the Border into Counties Tyrone and Fermanagh. The last native red deer disappeared from Co. Donegal in the mid 1800s. The Glenveigh Deer Park was created in 1891 when 23,000 acres were enclosed within a 28-mile deer fence around Slieve Snaght Mountain. The stock was originally Scottish hill deer but was supplemented over the years with English park stock. The fence broke several times over the years and deer spread throughout the surrounding hills. Extensive afforestation in the area has allowed the deer to spread through much of the county and across into Forestry Commission plantations in the North. Security considerations on the northern side of the border meant that little deer control was done over a period of 30 years, allowing numbers to build and spread. The Northern side of the border in Co. Tyrone is also the site of a large sika population originating from both Baronscourt and Colebrooke estates. The two species now share common ground and there have been some reports of hybridization.

Co. Wicklow

It is generally accepted that native red deer went into steep decline in Wicklow, as elsewhere, from the early seventeenth century onwards. Some authorities claim that there were no red deer in the county from 1600 until the early 20th century, when escapees from Powerscourt are known to have repopulated the northern end of the county. This claim is based on a lack of references to red deer in Wicklow in the available historical literature, although their presence is noted in several other counties through to the late nineteenth century.

Alternatively we may say that, in the absence of proof of extinction, red deer may well have survived, albeit in highly localised and small populations, through to the early 20th century, especially given that there were a number of deer parks throughout Wicklow, Wexford and Carlow from the mid seventeenth to the late nineteenth century, from which occasional escapes of both red and fallow deer may have augmented any remaining stock in Wicklow, facilitating a toehold until their scant numbers were given a fillip in the 1920s, and their survival underwritten, by deer from Powerscourt.

For many years they existed on the open mountain around the Sally Gap area, gradually extending southwards, at the same time as sika deer were also spreading, helped considerably by widespread planting of forests. Though hybridization had previously occurred within the confines of the park, widespread persecution, particularly of red deer in the 1930s and 1940s, saw regular appearance of red/sika hybrids in the wild and once this process started total contamination of both species of deer was inevitable.

Commercial shooting of deer for venison accelerated the process from the early 1980s. The red-like hybrids, being open mountain deer, were particularly vulnerable to overshooting and the widespread road network in the mountains made them susceptible to illegal lamping at night. Numbers have increased slightly since the inception of the Wicklow Mountains National Park but the red-type characteristics of the remaining deer are very diluted. Body size is relatively small, deer tend to have more white than cream rump patches, red-like deer rarely sport antlers of more than eight points and even then look more sika-like than red-like in structure. Rarely will one see a group of red-like deer in Wicklow without sika-like deer within the group.

Co. Meath

The basis of this population is the Ward Union Staghounds based in Dunshaughlin, Co. Meath and formerly in Slane Castle and Ashbourne. This hunt follows the carted deer, that is to say, deer taken from the park and hunted until held at bay whereupon they are caught up again and

Red deer of imported genetic bloodlines are now feral in many parts of Ireland. The exceptional head on this wild red deer stag is evidence of his origins

returned to the park. From time to time individual carted deer eluded their pursuers and lived wild, in due course breeding. A thriving population has now developed extending from the Boyne Valley in Co. Meath into Co. Louth and south to north Co. Dublin and north Co. Kildare. These deer have impressive antler genetics, the park having imported bloodlines from Warnham Court in Sussex, England. Antler quality is helped greatly by the good quality feeding available in this fertile area of the country.

Co. Down

A similar situation exists in Co. Down where the Co. Down Staghounds hunted deer from their deer park in Monalto near Ballinahinch; a feral population now exists in this area.

Co. Galway

A substantial population of red deer has developed recently in Connemara on the western side of Co. Galway. There are two distinct sources of this population.

With the establishment of the Connemara National Park, it was decided in 1982 to deer-fence the park and translocate a group of native red deer from Co. Kerry to the area to try to protect the Kerry strain from the possibility of hybridization. Not long after they arrived some deer broke the fence and a wild population developed. A second group of red deer escaped in the early 1990s from an enclosure in the Maam Cross area, further south. These were of English Park bloodlines and have moved though extensive Coillte forestry east towards Lough Corrib. There is thought to be some linkage now between this population and the original group in the Letterfrack area.

With the onset of deer farming there have in recent years been releases of red deer, both deliberate and accidental, in other areas of the country. At present there are known to be small feral populations in Tipperary, Wexford, Carlow, Sligo and the Dublin Mountains. Typically, these localised populations are short-lived unless the deer have access to extensive woodland. A small group of Kerry red deer are to be found on Inishvicillaune, one of the Blasket Islands still in private ownership. They were introduced in 1980 and have done reasonably well since, new blood in the form of stags from Muckross having been introduced from time to time.

Red Deer Male: Stag
Red Deer Female: Hind
Red Deer Young: Calf

Red deer calves weighing about 6 kg. are born from late May until about the middle of June, though it is possible to get calves born later, particularly with first-time calving hinds. They are chestnut in colour, with cream spots across their backs. Hinds tend to have traditional calving areas, particularly in the open mountain situation. They leave the calf in thick cover, returning only a few times a day to suckle and clean it. Within two weeks the calf usually follows its mother for most of the day. By early autumn, the last traces of white spots are gone from the coat.

Red deer calf

Red deer have a well-defined social structure. Male and female deer live for most of the year as separate groups, coming together only during the rut or breeding season. The size of these single-sex groups will depend on the habitat. On the open mountain group size may be up to fifty animals but in the woodland situation five to ten may be a more likely number, this may be because feeding areas are better and more evenly distributed. Deer living in sheltered woodland, preferably oak or beech, with ample feeding and protected against extreme weather conditions, will have the advantage over deer living in more exposed conditions and sharing limited feeding with sheep.

Compared with sika or fallow deer, the habits of red deer make them relatively easy to see, count, assess and manage on open ground. The hind is the mainstay of the family unit and each group, whatever its size, tends to have a lead hind. Male calves usually stay as part of the group until their first rut as prickets. The hind

Red deer stag in newly established coniferous plantation

group tends to have the same territory, usually the best grazing, all year round and the stags tend to move into this area during the rut. Dominance among the hinds is often settled by 'boxing', when they rear up on their back legs, striking out with their forelegs, to settle disputes regarding seniority. Hinds will bark when frightened or suspicious, this has the effect of alerting the other animals in the group to a potential threat. Sometimes they can alert the others in the group by just pricking their ears or stamping a forefoot. The only other noise that they make is an occasional squeaking, in communication with their calves.

Vital statistics of red deer vary widely, depending on their genetic background. Park type deer in Co Meath or on virgin territory in Co Galway will generally have higher body size and weights than woodland deer from Donegal, mountain red deer of Co. Kerry or the genetically compromised hybrid reds of Co Wicklow. However the following are guidelines (weights shown are live weights, not carcase weights):

Red stag: Shoulder height 1.2 metres. Weight 150kg
Red hind: Shoulder height 1.1 metres. Weight 100kg

This species of deer gets its name from the red or reddish brown colour of the coat in the summer months, being a light creamy colour inside the back legs. The summer coat is very short. Like all deer species there is a marked difference between the summer and winter coats. They have a 6-inch-long tail and a cream rump patch. In September the animal moults to its winter coat, which is grey-brown in colour. The spring moult from winter to summer coat is accompanied by a very scruffy appearance as it falls away over a couple of weeks.

'Hybrid red deer' hinds in summer coat. Note faint spotting

There are marked changes in the male during the rut. The neck thickens and a mane develops. There is staining of the hair of the underbelly in front of the penis where the animal urinates on itself. These changes get more pronounced as the animal gets older but each year they disappear when the rut ends. There is a characteristic odour associated with a red deer in the rut, which can often alert the stalker to its presence long before it is seen.

The rutting stag roars, a distinctive deep sound that can travel over long distances, particularly on the open hill. This main bellow may be accompanied by a number of loud hoarse grunts. The red deer hybrids of Co Wicklow make a sound which has been described as a cross between the red deer roar and the sika stag's rutting whistle. Outside the rut, male deer tend to make little if any noise. The red deer rut usually runs from the end of September until the beginning of November.

Under Irish conditions the red deer hind will normally conceive in the rut of her second year at around sixteen months of age, thereby calving at two years of age. In the harsher climate of the Scottish Highlands this may be delayed until the hind is three or even four years. The pregnancy length is 240 days and should a hind not be mated while in oestrus, she will usually come into heat again 21 days later.

Red deer hinds in winter coat

Each spring, red deer moult their winter coat and for stags, new antler growth starts

It should be possible to arrive at an educated guess as to the likely age of an animal by studying its shape. The young male aged from three to six years has a straight back, a balanced body and carries its head erect. As he ages, the body becomes more concentrated in the forequarters, particularly during the rut. The antlers eventually regress with age, showing a less developed outline and shape, often losing the crown. The gait of a healthy young stag is rhythmic and paced with head erect. At a gallop or fast run, or under trees, the head is carried thrown back.

Red deer hinds normally conceive at sixteen months of age

The hind has fewer but just as recognisable outward signs of aging; her body will thicken with age, her coat becoming duller and her flanks bonier. The skull is also heavier and nose apparently longer, her ears will be carried thrown back, as compared with a younger female, whose pronounced ears will usually be carried forward, especially when alert.

Hybrid stags can have rump patchs ranging from cream to pure white in colour

Eight point 'red' hybrid stag and hybrid pricket, with sika-type deer in foreground. Note size differential

CHAPTER IV

SIKA DEER

*Identification and Distribution: - History in Ireland – Distribution
- Particulars of the rut - -Hybridisation - International importance of Kerry sika*

In 1860 the seventh Lord Powerscourt introduced Japanese sika deer, Cervus nippon Nippon, to his estate near Enniskerry in Co Wicklow. From there they have spread around these islands, the process of which was described by Powerscourt himself:

> *'I bought one male and three females of this species from Jamrach, and my herd increased so much that I sold and gave away some, in the first place to the late Mr Herbert of Muckross, Killarney, and afterwards to Sir Croker Barrington at Glenstal, near Limerick: Sir Victor Brooke at Colebrooke, Co. Fermanagh, from whence they have spread to the Duke of Abercorn's woods at Baronscourt, Lord Dartrey's place in Co Monaghan and other places in the north of Ireland.'*

Sika deer are indigenous to eastern Asia, the Japanese islands, Taiwan and the mainland from Manchuria down to Vietnam. In fact the word 'sika' is Japanese for deer.

Sika stag with hinds, Killarney

In total there are fourteen separate subspecies. There are six of these subspecies on the Japanese islands. What we call Japanese sika are thought to be the subspecies found on Kyushu Island in Japan, first identified by Temninck in 1838.

One of the differences between the subspecies found on the Japanese islands and the others is that they have black velvet on their growing antlers, the other sika subspecies, such as Manchurian and Formosan sika common in some deer parks in the UK, all have red velvet antler. There are other differences in size and coat colouration.

There are three distinct populations of sika in Ireland.

Co. Wicklow

These deer, which originated in Powerscourt, spread slowly at first through the mountains of north Wicklow, when the park fence fell into disrepair. In 1934 Dr Peter Delap, writing in The Irish Naturalist's Journal, reported that there some 500-600 sika in the deer park at Powerscourt and a small group of about 50 deer living in the hills around Djouce, but that at that time, sika were not yet evident elsewhere outside Powerscourt. However it was when the State forestry plantations of the then Department of Lands were initiated that sika started to spread south and westwards.

They have at this stage reached very high densities in the Wicklow area, numbering an estimated 10-15,000 animals. They have spread to most of the counties of south Leinster including Dublin, Kildare, Carlow and Kilkenny – spreading relatively quickly where there are areas of interconnecting forestry.

Sika stag bedded down in brambles

Hybridisation with red deer is endemic in this population. Whereas the upland open hill deer in the county still show remarkable variation in hybrid characteristics, this is not so in the sika-type deer of the forestry plantations and in particular those animals on the edge of the expanding range. These animals are almost exclusively sika-like, having very few of the characteristics of red deer. While they look like pure Japanese sika they are not. They have a much larger body size and proportionately bigger antlers. There is an apparent tendency for sika genes to dominate where hybridisation occurs.

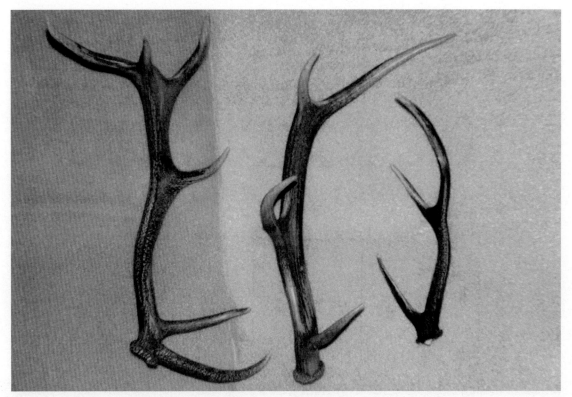

Red deer at left, sika deer at right. Antler of hybrid deer at centre, showing shared characteristics of red and sika

Co. Kerry

A stag and two hinds were introduced from Powerscourt to the Kenmare estate in 1865, where they rapidly increased in numbers. Further sika were introduced in the 1890s (two stags and five hinds from the Lansdowne Estate in Scotland, progeny from stock that originated from Powerscourt). They have now spread throughout Kerry and into many forests throughout west Cork.

The Co. Kerry sika are of importance because they are believed to be of 'pure' Japanese blood, having been moved from Wicklow before hybridization occurred there. With most of the sika worldwide showing signs of cross-breeding between red deer and other sika deer subspecies, the Co. Kerry Japanese sika may be of international significance. These sika deer are heavily shot within the boundaries of Killarney National Park, the main red deer range, to reduce the risk of hybridization.

Counties Tyrone & Fermanagh

Sika were first introduced to Colebrooke Park in Co. Fermanagh in 1870, where they were kept alongside a pre-existing herd of red deer. A number of hybrids of the two species were observed in the Park in 1885 and 1887. About 20 years later, some of the Colebrooke sika were moved to Baronscourt in Co. Tyrone, where they were kept in an enclosure. Both Parks are long since disbanded but the deer now range widely over Tyrone and south Fermanagh. There were definite hybrids noted in the wild sika population in 1973 when a male red deer from Donegal lived amongst the sika for three years.

Characteristic rump patch of sika deer, seen here in summer coat

Other areas

Sika deer are increasing in numbers and extending at the edge of their range. Stags wander furthest and are first to colonize new areas of forestry, often with regular disturbance hastening their spread. However there are reports of sika deer occurring in Galway, Mayo and Tipperary, unlikely to have occurred by natural expansion, suggesting human assistance at some level.

Sika Deer Male: Stag
Sika Deer Female: Hind
Sika Deer Young: Calf

Japanese sika deer are the smallest of our three deer species, with a marked difference in coat colour between summer and winter. There are also marked coat differences in the various degrees of hybridization between sika and red deer. In this chapter all details relate to pure Japanese sika unless otherwise stated.

The summer coat is chestnut brown with white spots. In areas where the two species are found together it is sometimes possible to confuse sika with common coloured fallow deer. Sika have erectile hairs on their white caudal patch. When alarmed, this patch of hair will flare to two or three times its normal size. This is an alarm mechanism to alert other deer in the group to a potential threat. This white caudal disc is surrounded by black hairs but unlike the cream caudal disc of red deer, it does not run up onto the rump. The tail is relatively short compared with fallow deer.

In September, sika moult from summer to winter coat. The moulting process starts on the neck and appears to work back along the flanks. This is because of the longer winter hair on the neck. Both hinds and stags are grey in the winter. The stag's coat is slightly darker but their wallowing habits at this time of year make them appear almost black in colour. The dark mane present in males during the rut is not as prominent as in the red deer stag because the hairs are proportionally shorter and the rest of the body is dark and so it is not as evident. The sika stag has a distinctive 'V' shape to the forehead, formed by lighter-coloured hair on the forehead. Males and females have distinctive rounded ears which differentiate them from the two other Irish deer species. The species also has a distinctive white colouration to the hair covering the metatarsal glands.

Sika hind and calf. The erectile hairs have flared on the calf's rump patch, causing the surrounding black hairs to disappear

Caudal patches and prominent metatarsal gland hairs, characteristic of sika deer

Stags are compact in build, with heavy shoulders. The typical mature sika stag has an eight point head, four points on either antler. Brow tines are upright rather than at right angles to the main beam, as with red deer. Whereas feeding has an important part to play in the size of antlers, genetics are important. The heads of Wicklow sika tend to be stronger and heavier than sika elsewhere, perhaps reflecting presence of red deer genes. Wicklow heads develop from six to eight points at an earlier age than, for example, the sika of Co. Kerry, where a six point head is regarded as the norm and more typical of 'pure' sika deer.

The other factor determining antler size is age. With increased culling, antler quality has declined markedly in some areas of Wicklow. Traditionally, stalkers have focussed on shooting male deer, facilitated by a longer season and more clement weather conditions. Male deer therefore lack the time and opportunity to achieve maturity and to develop antler quality. More emphasis must be given to culling females. Such a switch of emphasis facilitates better overall control of numbers while giving males time to mature and to develop the desired antler quality.

Japanese sika deer in Killarney (summer coat). Note velvet on growing antlers

Antlers are cast at the end of March, long before which the stags will have banded together into summer groups.

Sika stag: Shoulder height 0.9 metres. Weight 65kg
Sika hind: Shoulder height 0.8 metres.   Weight 45kg

Sika calves are born from late May onwards. In general there is quite a spread over the calving period. Newborn calves can frequently be found from September into October. Whereas most sika hinds come into heat in the October of their second year and calve at two years of age, studies in the UK have proven exceptional fertility amongst sika hinds. Pregnancy rates have been demonstrated at 90% in adult females, 80% in yearling females and 12% in calves. For calves to become pregnant they must attain a critical weight and are unlikely to reach that before late winter. An October born calf would have been conceived in February. With early-stage pregnancies difficult to detect by the average stalker and the end of the season being the end of February, these calf pregnancies often go unnoticed.

Twinning is rare and difficult to prove as a hind can feed two calves but that does not mean that both were born to her. There have however been several reports of twin foetuses in the Co. Wicklow area.

Although very rare in Irish deer species, twinning can occur, as evidenced by these twin foetuses from a sika hind

Sika hind in summer coat

The calves are born with a spotted coat not unlike that of the red calf, which they lose with the onset of autumn. They suckle for at least sixteen weeks and while they should be self-sufficient by November with the opening of the hind culling season, research suggests that calves deprived of their mother at any time between early life and spring of the following year are unlikely to survive. Stalkers should always endeavour to shoot the calf before shooting any accompanying hind.

Traditionally sika deer were thought to have a preference for areas of acid soil type - such as heather uplands, coniferous forests and rhododendron thickets - but they are extremely adaptable and do well in almost any habitat. Like all our deer species they are basically grazers but will browse as well. Thicket areas of conifer forest are most likely to be colonized. They do most of their damage on newly planted ground but actually spend relatively little time in these areas.

In areas where there is little available feeding, particularly in the winter and the spring, and disturbance levels are high, they are responsible for severe browsing damage to young trees and for bark stripping in semi-mature plantations. Bole scoring, the ripping off of bark with antlers, a common trait of sika deer in the UK, is relatively rare in Ireland but it does occur.

The sika rut is the same as that for red deer, from the end of September to the beginning of November. Stags can be very aggressive, chasing and fighting other stags and thrashing vegetation, though immature males are tolerated in a territory. This aggressive nature often results in broken antlers. This is particularly evident in some areas such as Co. Kerry, where there may be an added problem of poor mineralisation of antlers.

Mature stags have definite rutting areas. They regularly patrol these territories, wallowing in boggy areas, scraping with their feet and thrashing small trees in the general areas. Sika in hill or moorland areas often adopt mating behaviour more often associated with red deer, in that they collect hinds and try to hold them in a harem.

Sika stag prepares to mount a hind in Killarney National Park

They increase their scenting of the area by urinating into their wallows. When the hinds come into season the stag will sniff her vulva and lick her urine.

The sika stag makes a characteristic triple whistle sound during the rut, but occasionally the number may vary. One stag whistling very often stimulates another to whistle nearby. This vocal activity is primarily from dusk to just after dawn, but in the peak of the rut it may continue all day. Whistling frequency increases when the weather is cold. The rutting whistle of the sika stag can be heard from the end of August, long before any hinds come into season. Stags also make a low mewing sound during the rut, though this will only be heard when the stalker is quite close. Sika stags constantly scent-mark their territories.

Sika stag in winter coat

CHAPTER V

FALLOW DEER

Identification and Distribution - History in Ireland – Distribution
Particulars of the rut - Different colour forms

Fallow deer (Dama dama) are not native to Ireland but are the most widespread of our three deer species. They are thought to have been introduced by the Normans to the 'Royal Deer Forest' of Glencree, Co. Wicklow in 1244. They were then spread over the centuries to numerous deer parks throughout the country. Examination of maps shows many place names relating to deer parks. A good number of these parks fell into disrepair many years ago and the deer escaped to nearby forests where they thrived, due mainly to the widespread natural hardwood afforestation which marked the Irish countryside through the period of plantation and clearance from the middle of the seventeenth century. Many more were abandoned around the time of independence in the early part of the last century and more recently there have been new wild populations resulting from deer farm escapees.

Common-coloured fallow buck in early winter coat – from a high seat

Fallow are members of the genus Dama rather than Cervus, which includes red and sika deer. The main difference between these groups is that deer of the Dama group produce palmated antlers, lack a mane in the rut and have no upper canine teeth. There are two members of this genus, the European fallow deer and the Mesopotamian or Persian form, an endangered subspecies which is only found in the wild in Israel and in a few isolated areas of Iran. Though endangered, a number of the Mesopotamian-European hybrids were introduced to Ireland and used as sires on fallow deer farms, to increase body size. There is always a danger that some of these hybrids could escape and pollute our fallow gene pool. Though a bigger animal, these crosses do not have the wide antler palmation that we associate with fallow deer.

Unlike our other two deer species, it is difficult to define definite regions in the country where they are to be found. They are widely distributed both in the Republic and Northern Ireland. They tend not to travel widely and are still concentrated very much in the areas where they originally escaped, even in some cases after many centuries. As will be described later, there are several colour variations of fallow deer; some or all will be found in these different populations, probably dependant on the colour preference (if any) of the owner of the original park.

The major populations of fallow deer are Laois/Offaly, Tipperary/Waterford, Clare, Galway, Wicklow, Monaghan/Louth/Armagh, Fermanagh, Down, Roscommon around Lough Key and Sligo/Leitrim around Lough Gill. However in each county, the populations are often distinct, with little if any mixing between them. For example there are a number of distinct areas with fallow deer in Co Galway, including Portumna, Ballygar and Mountbellew.

Fallow deer are larger than Japanese sika deer but equate in height and size to the sika-like deer to be found in the Wicklow region. Fallow have a longer tail than the other species and their ears are long and pointed.

Fallow buck browsing in broadleaf woodland,
in this case on a mature tree

Fallow are predominantly grazers but will browse, particularly on bramble during the winter months. They can cause considerable damage in young broadleaf woodland, eating the leaders and side shoots, and also in agricultural crops. In more mature blocks a large number of fallow will create an obvious browse line. The movement from forestry to open feeding areas is usually along well-marked tracks. The species has become almost nocturnal in their grazing habits in areas of high disturbance, however in their preferred habitat of mixed pole-stage and semi-mature woodland, there are usually enough secluded places to graze undisturbed and a good understory of cover for lying up. Fallow may vacate an area completely in areas of high disturbance or widespread felling, but reappear in following years when conditions settle. Like our other species, fallow deer are gregarious, though both bucks and does live in separate herds for most of the year, with the exception of the rutting period. More so than red or sika, fallow are particularly sensitive to changes in weather, and are unlikely to be visible in the open in wet or windy weather.

Fallow Deer Male: Buck (shoulder height 1.0 metre, approximate weight 100kg)
Fallow Deer Female: Doe (shoulder height 0.85 metres, approximate weight 45kg)
Fallow Deer Young: Fawn

Fallow bucks in hard horn, late summer.
Note prominent Adam's Apple,
penile sheath and tail

Males

Male fallow deer can be distinguished from females as young fawns by the presence of long hairs on the end of the penile sheath, which grow further as they mature. Pedicles first appear around eight months of age. Fallow prickets can sometimes be difficult to recognize by novice stalkers, as sometimes the antler development is very small, with only very small buttons developing. The more experienced will instantly recognise a male by the shape of the body, particularly as the rut approaches and the neck starts to swell. There is no mane development. Bucks have a very pronounced larynx or Adam's apple.

Fallow deer antlers are palmate in shape, rather than carrying a given number of tines on a main beam. While they have brow tines and the equivalent of the red deer's trey tine, the latter just below the beginning of the palmation, the antler then sweeps up in a curve. It is wider at the top than the bottom and is backed by protuberances of antler known as spellers. In a mature buck there should often be a rear-facing tine. In general, wild fallow do not develop palms until about four years of age.

Centuries of culling for antler quality does not appear to have benefited Irish fallow bucks greatly and antler quality rarely equates to the best available in mainland Europe. Many suffer from fishtails, an indentation in the main beam which gives the appearance of a fishtail. Fallow bucks also suffer from the fact that they can spend a large amount of the early autumn grazing in the open. Most male fallow do not live long enough to produce the antlers that are considered typical for the species.

Fallow bucks move from their summering areas to ground permanently occupied by the does, where they take up rutting stands, usually in thick cover. Males do not normally hold a rutting stand until five or six years of age - and often older. In many areas in this country, male fallow deer are under extreme hunting pressure due to a long open season (formerly six months) and as a result there is often a shortage of mature males; in such circumstances younger bucks may well hold a rutting stand earlier than elsewhere.

Typical antler of mature fallow buck

The females then wander into these stands when in heat. Fallow deer tend not to hold does, as red deer stags usually do. During the rut, bucks make a distinctive repetitive grunting noise which sounds like a belch while on the stand. For the rest of the year they are generally silent. Around the stand the ground is often torn up - bucks scrape the ground with their feet and antlers and thrash the branches of nearby trees but they seldom wallow. During the rut, the neck swells and the end of the penis sheath and the flanks become stained. They urinate over themselves and also scent-mark surrounding vegetation from their suborbital glands. The same areas tend to be used for rutting by fallow deer year after year. Unlike other species of deer, fallow bucks can rarely be called off a stand by the stalker.

Fallow deer rutting stand in mixed forest

Rutting activity consists of the continual parading of the stand area with occasional periods of grunting. Bucks eat little or nothing during this period; consequently they lose weight and are usually unable to defend their territory for much more than one to two weeks, after which time an otherwise subordinate buck may commandeer the stand.

Females

Parkland fallow does exhibit their gracefulness on the run

Does occasionally bark if alarmed and mewing is commonly heard, particularly when deer are moving. It is a gentle communication between doe and fawn. In general it is assumed that 70% of fallow does will bring a fawn through the winter, before any cull is considered, illustrating the necessity for hard culling just to maintain the local herd at a static figure.

Colour Variations

There are five main colour variations in Irish fallow deer. The fact that there is variation at all in this species is an indication that they have been inbred in parks, semi-domesticated, for many centuries.

Common

As the name suggests, this is the colour form seen most frequently in wild populations. In summer it is a rich brown colour dappled with white spots on the upper flanks and with a black stripe running from a point in the middle of the back down to the tip of the tail, broadening as it goes. The chest and belly, and the underside of the neck, are distinctly white in summer. In winter this colour form becomes darker, almost donkey-brown in appearance, with the summer spots virtually disappearing. The broad stripe along the back in the summer coat becomes less obvious as it merges with the winter colouring. As with all deer, the summer coat is much shorter and glossier, making the definition of all spots and lines more obvious.

This group of fallow bucks, photographed in Dublin's Phoenix Park, show all fallow deer colour variations except white

Menil

The menil colouration is basically a paler version of common pelage. All the black areas in the common animal are replaced with a pale brown. Spots are retained in the winter coat. There are various hues of the menil form. They are a popular form in deer parks. The genetics of coat colour in fallow are complex but suffice to say here that mating two menil deer will always produce a menil fawn. While many of these park deer escaped with the other forms, they

Group of menil fallow deer in winter coat

have disappeared in a good deal of our wild populations as their relatively bright colour has made them particularly vulnerable to hunters. Menil bucks have a very pale antler velvet, unlike that of the other colour forms mentioned above.

Black

Black fallow, also known as melanistic, are the darkest form. Whereas the coat is completely black in the winter, there are faint brown spots on the coat in the summer. There is no obvious rump spot.

White

Not a frequent colouration in wild Irish fallow, though seen in some populations in Waterford and Tipperary. They are often kept in parks in pure white herds. This colouration also breeds true. Two pure white fallow deer herds are to be found in parks in Mallow, Co. Cork and Parkanaur in Co. Tyrone. The fawns are initially born with a sandy-coloured coat and turn paler with each succeeding moult, eventually turning white at about three years of age. White fallow are not albinos, which are characterized by having pink unpigmented eyes.

White fallow deer at Parkanaur, Co. Tyrone

Brown

The brown form was often considered as black as both are dark in winter, however there is a marked difference in summer coat as they are a distinctive dark brown colour. A black line is visible down the back and around the heart-shaped rump spot.

There are other variations of coat in fallow deer which have not as yet been reported in this country. There is a blue form (in reality, grey) found in Woburn Park, Bedfordshire, England and a longhaired variety, common in colour with a shaggy coat and tufts of hair growing out of each ear, found in Shropshire, England.

CHAPTER VI

DEER STALKING AIDS AND TECHNIQUES

*High seat design and use – Binoculars – Clothing – Knives - Dogs for deer stalking -
Aiming points - Reaction to the shot - Dealing with a wounded animal*

HIGH SEATS FOR DEER SHOOTING

The use of high seats for deer shooting is well established in Britain and across continental Europe but is seldom practised in Ireland. To some extent this reflects the nature of the quarry species in other countries, such as roe deer, muntjac or Chinese water deer, for which the stalking season is normally much more clement than for species such as red, sika or fallow; also being woodland deer, roe especially are more difficult to stalk in heavy summer woodland. Any stalking environment with limited security of tenure and limited control of long term planning of deer management also militates against their use.

A well constructed high seat, with a wide field of view

However high seats have a definite value for stalking and are recommended where possible or practical to erect. They allow for the safest possible shot, always downward and with a definite backstop in the form of the ground. Also, properly sited, they allow for careful study and observation of the ground and for greater selectivity of quarry. They are especially useful in situations where at ground level young trees obliterate the view, or on flat land, or where public usage is high and margins of safety are low. High seats increase the observer's visibility over the trees and provide a comfortable and stable shooting position and allowing a safer shooting angle towards the ground. High seats also lift the stalker out of the deer's scent field. For these reasons, and especially where the stalker has a medium or long-term commitment to deer control on designated ground, the installation of high seats is highly recommended.

High seats offer a wide view and a safe backdrop for shooting. The fallow deer seen in the centre of this photograph may not have been visible from ground level

Installation on Coillte Teoranta forest property is subject to approval and authorisation, which can normally be obtained through the local forester for the area concerned.

There are a variety of basic designs for construction which can be followed, ranging from a freestanding tower to a simple tree-supported ladder.

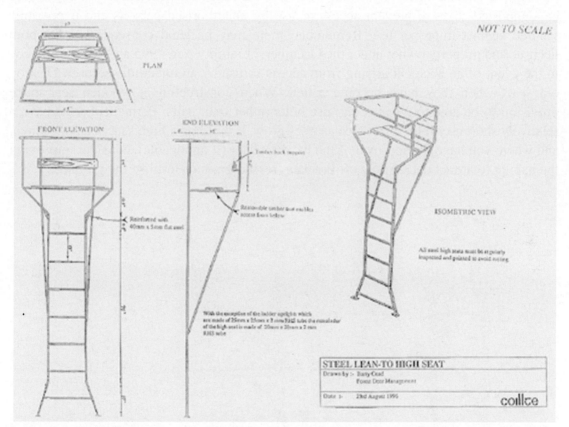

Coillte-designed high seat (steel)

Siting is critical. The seat should be erected where it affords the best field of view over known deer territory, where deer feed or over which they cross regularly. Reconnaissance is needed and will pay dividends. There will be plenty of suitable places in a forest, so try not to site it anywhere where there will be too much public access. There are few things more frustrating than to be sitting quietly in a high seat for a couple of hours only to have some hill walkers stroll by beneath you.

A low seat will provide a safe rested shot in many situations

Once the site is chosen and authorisation obtained, the type of seat to be erected can be decided. A "low" seat can be as effective as a "high" seat, i.e. as a seat at ground level, provided the key requirement of safety is secured.

Once erected, high seats must be properly maintained to ensure safety. Only treated timbers should be used and worn or rotting timbers should be replaced annually. Staple chicken-wire over the rungs for added safety. They should be signposted so as to prevent access or use by unauthorised persons and if possible, secured against improper use. Remember, there may be legal consequences for both licensee and property owner under the Occupiers' Liability Act, 1995 and at common law in the event of an accident arising from access or use by an unauthorised user. Destroy old seats when they have become rotten. When constructing a wooden seat make provision to be able to move it e.g. use bolts rather than nails. Permanent seats have a relatively short useful life in an area as trees grow. If building a high seat in an open area, and where you have the approval of the local forester (if applicable), consider improving the habitat to attract deer. Spray off bracken, reseed grass or fertilise the ground.

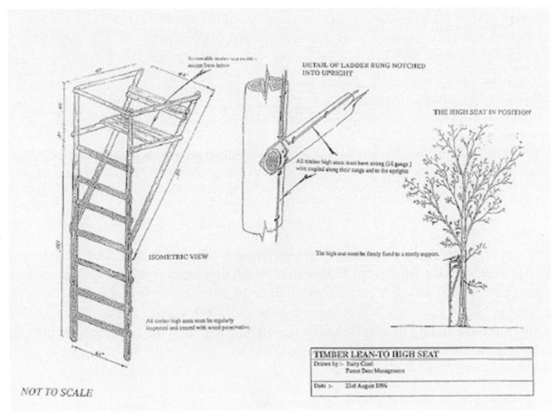

Coillte-designed high seat (timber

The stalker must not be silhouetted in a high seat. Free-standing high seats should be boxed in and preferably roofed. Lean-to high seats should ideally be set against a background of trees, preferably with some screening around the shooting rail.

High seats are particularly useful for the culling of fallow deer, which are difficult to stalk where bracken and brambles abound. Fallow often follow distinct tracks through the wood and seats should be sited nearby. Be careful not to place it too near to where you expect deer to appear. If a seat is sited deep in a forest then deer will be seen from it for a long period of the day, particularly in the autumn. Building a seat in a totally open area will limit the time at which it is useful, to dawn and dusk.

Consideration should be given to the route of access to a high seat. Clear branches and twigs from the path that you intend to use. If using it in the evening arrive at least one hour before you expect the deer to move. When sitting in a seat you will notice that visibility is enhanced by removing branches from one or two nearby trees, or even chopping down one or two small trees. When getting permission to erect the seat check first that the landowner or forester has no objection to you pruning branches or opening up the field of view.

Portable metal ladder-type seats are available commercially but provide little shelter or comfort in inclement weather conditions. On the other hand, they can be re-located relatively quickly. If left on site between visits to the stalking ground, they should be secured against theft.

BINOCULARS

Binoculars are an essential tool in stalking. Without them, the stalker's prospects of seeing wild deer in time to do anything about them are limited. As with telescopic sights, emphasis should be on quality of manufacture, including quality of lenses. The manufacturers of the best telescopic sights also make the best binoculars.

There are two choices as to type of binocular: "Porro" prism or roof prism. The "Porro" prism takes its name from its Italian inventor. It uses two prisms set at right angles to each other between the objective lens and the eyepiece. Porro's original design was perfected at the end of the 19th century and it has changed little since then.

8 x 40 Porro prism binoculars   *8 x 42 Roof prism binoculars*

Porro prism binoculars were standard until the 1960s, when the roof prism was introduced. With roof prism binoculars, the objective lenses are straight in line with the eyepieces. Roof prism binoculars are compact, light and comfortable to hold. Compared with roof prism binoculars, Porro prisms can look and feel old-fashioned and heavy but they are still highly serviceable and have the advantage of being considerably less expensive than roof prism binoculars.

Every pair of binoculars is identified with a formula such as "7 x 42" or "8 x 56". The first number in the formula is the power, or how many times the image is enlarged. With hand held binoculars, there is a practical limit to power, beyond which it is not useful. Depending on the individual, as the power increases, hand tremor begins to degrade the image. Binoculars over 10 power usually require tripod mounting.

The second number in the formula is the diameter of the objective lens in millimetres. The bigger the objective, the more light can enter and the greater the potential resolution of the image.

Low-light performance is largely dependent on the exit pupil. Exit pupils are the small, bright circles you see in the eyepieces when you hold binoculars away from your eyes and up to the light. They are the actual beams of light coming out through the eyepieces. The exit pupil is calculated by dividing the diameter of the objective lens by the power. A 7 x 35 binocular has an exit pupil of 5 millimetres ($35 \div 7 = 5$). A 10 x 32 binocular has an exit pupil of 3.2 millimetres ($32 \div 10 = 3.2$).

In bright light, the pupils of the eyes contract to 2 to 4 m.m., and at night they may open to 7 m.m. If the beam of light exiting the binoculars is wider than the pupil of the eye, the excess doesn't get in: the eye can't see it. During daylight hours things look just as bright through binoculars with 4 mm exit pupils as through those with 7 m.m. exit pupils. It is in low light that the larger exit pupil is an advantage. For stalking in low light conditions therefore, an exit pupil of 6 to 7 m.m. is recommended. Good stalking configurations include 7 x 42 (small, light and very portable) or 8 x 56 (bigger, heavier and less portable but best in poor light).

Field of view

"Field of view" describes the width of the area encompassed in the binoculars' image. It can be expressed as an angle (8°), or as the width in feet of the image at 1000 yards (420 ft.). To convert the angular field to the linear field, multiply the angular field by 52.5. Field of view is a matter of eyepiece design. More power usually means a narrower field of view. Wide-field-of-view eyepieces usually have shorter eye relief and may not work for eyeglass wearers.

Binoculars should ideally be rubber-armoured, the colour of the rubber being immaterial. Both lenses should be fitted with covers to protect against rain.

Some stalkers will also use a telescope, either fixed or draw barrel, and there is no doubt that a telescope offering up to 30 power magnification can be invaluable over long distances on open ground. However not everyone can use a telescope to full advantage, and they are both heavy and unwieldy to carry while stalking. On balance, the Irish stalker will not benefit greatly by having a stalking telescope. The modern spotting scope can be useful and is less unwieldy than the telescope. It is mounted on a small tripod and can be useful to examine an animal from a distance, to save a long detour on a stalk.

When stalking in woodland the cardinal rule is to walk slowly and use the binoculars often. Every couple of paces opens up a whole new vista to be examined. Here a pair of low power binoculars with a relatively wide field of view is important. Autofocus binoculars are invaluable in this situation. They allow both the foreground and background to be in focus at the same time. It is important that the stalker shouldn't have to spend too much time fiddling to find focus – particularly with a rifle on the shoulder and a stalking stick in the other hand.

CLOTHES

Although the Irish stalker is not yet burdened with the necessity of wearing American-style fluorescent "hunter blaze" clothing, such clothing may not be such a bad idea, especially if stalking with others, or likely to encounter other hunters in dense or dark forest conditions. Meanwhile, the essential requirements are merely that your chosen apparel should be practical, comfortable, weatherproof, silent and from the deer's point of view, blend with the stalker's physical surroundings.

Camouflage or hunter blaze? Both in this case!

There are many proprietary brands of clothing to choose from, including modern materials and treatments which have to some extent displaced the waxed cotton once a favourite for all-weather stalking in difficult conditions. Wool and tweed remain traditional choices but are heavy when wet and often too warm for early-season stalking. However if using a high seat, weight is not a consideration and the stalker may be grateful for added warmth. Camouflage cotton can be useful but should be of a treated fabric, both to reduce noise and to ensure weatherproofing.

Denim is to be avoided as moisture will travel directly up from the trouser cuff and quickly reach the nether regions, even from wet grass.

Camouflage gear may be appropriate in some circumstances

A face veil will hide a white face

Heat loss is fastest through the head and wrists, making a hat essential and gloves or at least wrist cuffs recommended. A scarf is also recommended in cold weather, to keep the back of the neck warm.

In thick woodland where deer may be encountered at close quarters, or when sitting on a high seat, a face veil and gloves are recommended. The white of hands moving up and down with a pair of binoculars will soon alert any nearby deer.

FOOTWEAR

Footwear is largely a matter of personal choice but must be practical and safe. Rubber Wellington boots or composite leather-and-rubber boots are popular choices. If stalking in forestry, sound is a key factor and studded soles may prove a disadvantage. If stalking on rocky or hilly terrain, good ankle support is essential.

The final choice of clothing and footwear must rest with the wearer and will depend on stalking conditions – including seasonal factors, weather conditions and nature of stalking ground.

Hunting on rough terrain, good ankle support is important

KNIVES

The stalker's knife is first and foremost a working tool, and must be capable of bleeding, gralloching, skinning and jointing an animal. The blade can be fixed or folding, and need not have a cutting edge longer than three to four inches. If using a folding knife, choose a locking type – and make sure that it locks securely in the open position. A drop-point hollow-ground blade is recommended. The drop-point design is based on a blade tip lowered (dropped) via a convex arc from the spine or back of the blade. It allows for a strong point and a general controllability of the knife, a useful characteristic when hands are cold or wet. The hollow grind is done by taking two concave scoops out of the side of the blade. The advantage of this design is that the edge is extraordinarily thin, and thin edges slice better. The disadvantage is that the thinner the edge, the weaker it is. Hollow ground edges can chip or roll over in harder use. A hollow-ground blade should not be used for cutting bone as this will damage the cutting edge.

'Buck' hollow-ground hunting knife with drop-point blade

Many hunting knives are hollow ground, because field dressing is often best done with a knife that slices exceptionally well through soft tissues. Another advantage of the hollow ground knife is ease of sharpening. Most hollow grinds thicken slightly towards the edge. That means that as you sharpen, the blade gets thinner and easier to sharpen. With time, however, the blade begins thickening non-linearly and sharpening will become more difficult.

'Buck' hollow-ground hunting/skinning knife with 'gut hook' or gralloching blade

The stalker should not need to use his knife other than for cutting flesh or hide, and a heavy knife with six or seven inch blade is unnecessary, as well as being extra weight to carry on the hill. A keen cutting edge is essential, and most hollow-ground stalking knives will require honing after every use. A carborundum stone with coarse and fine sides is best, used with a light oil and moving the knife edge in circles on the stone. Once the essential requirements of a practical knife are recognised, the stalker can choose from a wide selection of manufacturers, including many hand-made knives of superb quality. Weight, length, strength, grip and ability to hold and keep a keen cutting edge are the main factors to consider in choosing a knife.

Most stalkers will have at some time left a knife behind in a forest when eviscerating a deer, so consider using a tie or thong on the handle of the knife. If prone to losing things, it might be wise to carry a second knife. It is important to keep the stalking knife for use on the hill, and a proper set of skinning and butchering knives for use in the larder, together with a steel for sharpening. All knives should be properly washed after use.

Careless handling of knives can represent a serious safety hazard, both in use and if left lying around in an unguarded fashion. Learn to use your knife with prudence and care.

OTHER STALKING AIDS

A stalking stick will prove invaluable, not only as an aid to walking on difficult terrain, but equally as a shooting aid. The stick will be helpful when crossing streams, or negotiating a steep bank. It can also be used (standing, kneeling or sitting) to steady the barrel of the gun prior to shooting. Traditionally sticks were as long as the stalker is tall, of ash or holly and two to three inches in circumference, giving strength but not at the expense of weight. A fork top is useful, perhaps of antler, but make sure that the forks are rounded off and not sharp, as a fall with stick in hand could result in the loss of an eye. A useful modern variation is the double stalking stick, usually made of slim six-foot brown or green plastic coated bean poles, available from most garden centres, although proprietary versions are also available. They are bolted together at eye height and when opened will provide an often steadier rest than a single stick. Treble sticks that form an even steadier tripod are also available commercially. Care must be taken when stalking not to make noise by letting the stalking stick rattle against the rifle, and a rubber or horn 'shoe' on the end of the stick is essential.

Folding bipod

"Knobloch" rifle tripod

No stalker should venture on the hill without a working knowledge of the ground, and a familiarity with maps for the local area. On high ground a mist can fall quickly, shrouding every landmark and completely altering the lie of the land. A compass takes up little room in the pocket and could save a life, as could an emergency signal flare. A length of rope, light, strong but never thin, will greatly aid the inevitable drag of a carcase off the hill sooner or later.

DOGS FOR DEER STALKING

It is a condition of the Coillte Teoranta forest stalking permit that every licensee and nominated stalker must have access to a dog trained to follow up and locate a shot or wounded deer.

It is the dog's sense of smell which makes it invaluable in terms of tracking deer so while almost any dog can be trained for the purpose, the stalker is advised to stick to one of the recognised hunting breeds, such as the Labrador Retriever, or one of the popular Continental breeds such as the Teckel or the Bavarian Mountain Hound. The German Shorthaired Pointer and the German Wirehaired Pointer are increasing in popularity but remember, the primary function of these breeds is to range widely in search of game and like the Spaniel, must be properly trained to walk quietly at heel until called upon to search.

Labrador Retrievers

German Teckel. Photo: Deer-UK.com

The dog will be required to follow a blood trail and hopefully, bring the stalker to the deer where it has fallen, dead or alive. If alive, the stalker should immediately administer a coup de grace with his firearm. Given that even a fatally wounded deer can run for considerable distances, and very quickly disappear especially in heavy forestry, the advantages of an adequately trained dog will quickly become apparent to the regular stalker. It may be prudent to work less experienced dogs on a long leash when following a blood trail and allowing only more experienced dogs to hunt freely.

The chosen dog must be trained to walk silently at heel without the need to constantly recall to heel. He must drop instantly to the slightest command and remain seated for as long as necessary, while the stalker readies for and takes the shot. He must be steady to the shot and must not run in. The experienced dog will often indicate the presence of unseen deer by his reaction to scent. Ideally he will ignore all other game scent.

Bavarian Mountain Hounds. Photo: Deer-UK.com

The time and effort required to bring a dog to this standard of steadiness, obedience and competence is significant but once achieved the stalker will have an invaluable stalking assistant as well as a companion to be enjoyed for his contribution to sport.

In some European countries, the use of dogs in deerstalking has been brought to an advanced level but requires time, dedication and no little experience. In Germany, for example, training of the dog can go beyond basic training and the dog is expected to track the wounded, dead or dying deer and to return to its handler when found, showing by its attitude that it has found the animal and bringing the stalker to it. This is known as the *"Verweiser"* technique.

German Wire-Haired Pointers

"Bringselverweiser" is the next and more advanced stage of training, where the dog returns with the "bringsel" in its mouth to denote that it has found the animal dead. The bringsel is a short piece of wood or leather which is attached to the dog's collar. When the dog finds the animal, he should swing the bringsel into his mouth and return to his handler with the message that the animal is definitely down and dead.

"Totverbeller" describes the dog which barks or bells to his handler on finding the dead or dying deer, so that the handler can make his way to the barking dog and deal with the deer appropriately.

Totverbeller! German Pointer on wild boar

All training starts with teaching the dog to find and to follow a blood trail rather than merely a foot scent. To do this the handler will need a supply of fresh animal blood, preferably deer's blood. When collecting blood from a dead deer it should be mixed with salt, which will prevent it from clotting. It can then be frozen in small quantities, enough for each training session. Lay a trail by dragging a blood-soaked rag in a zigzag fashion across open ground. The best way to do this is to tie the rag onto a line and have a friend drag one end while you drag the other, so ensuring that the dog is not merely following your foot-trail. Lift the rag as you progress, so that it is touching the ground and depositing a spot of blood only every three or four feet to start, extending to three or four yards as the dog's training progresses. Ideally the objective of the trailing exercise should be a deer carcase but if this is not possible, use a deer skin (fresh or cured). Leave some morsel on the objective as a reward for the dog when he finds the object of his search. Use less blood over longer distances, wider areas and tougher terrain as training progresses.

The *"bringsel"* method is achieved by teaching the dog to retrieve the bringsel from the object of the search so that eventually he will retrieve it automatically once an animal is found. From there is a short progression to securing the bringsel so that it dangles from the collar and the dog learns to retrieve it by swinging it into his mouth, but only when he has found the object of the search.

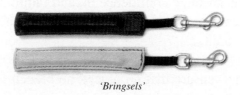

'Bringsels'

"Totverbeller" requires that the handler teach the dog to bark or "speak" on finding the object of his search. This is achieved by a) first teaching it to bark more or less on command and thereafter, b) teaching it to bark on finding the quarry. Start by teaching the dog to bark for his food, then on finding a piece of deer skin, moving gradually up the "search and find" scale of difficulty until the dog can search and find successfully and on finding the deer, bay, bark or bell to signal to his handler that he has found the quarry.

In Norway and Sweden, Elkhounds are trained in this fashion to find elk both living and wounded or dead i.e. to hunt the live unshot animal and to hold it at bay until the arrival of the shooter as well as tracking and holding the wounded animal or baying at the body of the dead elk. In Germany, Belgium and France the Bavarian Mountain Hound and other breeds are similarly trained for boar hunting as well as for tracking shot deer.

The handler may find it useful to attach a couple of small bells to the dog's collar before release on a trail. The sound of the bells will assist in knowing where the dog is, especially in heavy cover. The dog will quickly come to recognise the attachment of the bells as a signal that work is about to commence. Falconry bells are useful for this purpose; the small bells sometimes found on children's toys are also suitable.

Bringing a dog to this stage of training and excellence is a time-consuming task, requiring both skill and patience, but well worth the effort, adding greatly to efficiency and enjoyment. These notes on training are far from exhaustive but there are many excellent texts on dog training, widely available.

TAKING THE SHOT

It should be every stalker's objective to ensure a clean, efficient and humane kill, with minimum carcase damage. It follows that the stalker must deal with three specific areas before taking the shot. These are:

a) the rifle itself: the stalker must ensure that his rifle is up to the job – that it is safe and serviceable, of appropriate calibre and above all, that it is correctly zeroed at a range appropriate for the calibre and bullet load. Rifle maintenance and zeroing are covered separately within this training manual.

b) accuracy and safety: the stalker must be both capable and confident in his ability to place the round on target, and he must ensure that he has a safe field of fire and an adequate backstop before he attempts to take the shot. Shooting on or near farmland in particular, the stalker must make himself aware of the presence of any livestock or bloodstock. An unexpected rifle shot can easily cause a horse to bolt, causing injury or worse to itself or to its rider. Regular range practice is essential so that the stalker has absolute confidence in, and familiarity with, his firearm and he is capable of consistently placing the round within the designated and recommended target area.

Before taking the shot, ensure that no object, no branch or twig and especially no rock, boulder or other hard surface intervenes between muzzle of rifle and the quarry. Even the smallest twig or tussock can deflect the bullet and a ricochet can result from hitting any hard surface or even water. Take care to ensure that the bullet cannot travel through or beyond the target without a solid backstop to stop its flight and ensure too that no other deer stands behind the primary target. The stalker must ensure a steady rifle; a rested shot, preferably prone, is always best, otherwise the stalker should adopt one of the other recommended positions e.g. kneeling or supported by stick or tree. An off-hand unrested standing shot is to be avoided but if no other option is available, the stalker should adopt a well-practised standing shot, using the rifle sling to steady the rifle.

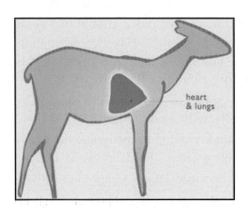 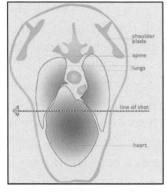

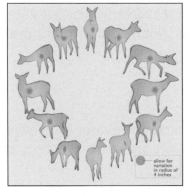 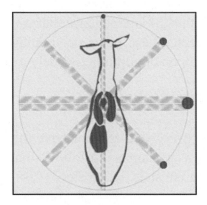

These "shot clock" schematics show the optimum area for bullet placement
(heart & lung shot) from different angles of fire, including from above.

c) The aiming point: there can be little doubt that the broadside heart and lung shot is the best shot to take in the field, having regard for the variety of circumstances which can arise. The heart and lung shot can be achieved other than in a broadside position, for example, when the deer faces the stalker frontally or when it stands facing away at an angle. There is also minimal meat damage and should the animal not fall where shot, the entry and/or exit wound will generate an adequate blood trail for you or your tracking dog to follow. However, an angled broadside shot is to be avoided with the smaller calibres such as .22/250.

Neck shots should be avoided if at all possible, even though in theory, they offer reduced carcase damage. With this shot, the target is the spinal cord – a relatively difficult target for even the most experienced marksman to hit consistently under field conditions. You may end up merely damaging the windpipe and gullet, to have the animal escape to die later, usually of starvation. Neck shots are a particular problem with male deer during the rut, when the neck swells but vital internal structures remain unchanged in size.

Headshots should not be taken. The killing zone is small and the slightest movement of the deer's head can result in severe damage to jaw, eyes or nose, leading to a lingering and painful death later.

Remember – the point is not to demonstrate your skill as a marksman; it is to achieve a clean, efficient and humane kill.

REACTIONS TO THE SHOT

The deer's bodily reaction to the shot will usually confirm where the bullet has struck. Typically, with a heart and lung shot, the deer will bound or lurch forward but it can still run up to a hundred metres before collapsing. Sika stags can sometimes run further. It may also lash out with its hind legs before running off. However this shot, especially taken with the deer broadside to the shooter, will yield a distinct bright red blood trail if shot though the heart, or a white-specked frothy blood trail if shot through the lungs. These are usually easy to follow and the deer can, with confidence, be expected to be found dead.

A successful neck shot, severing the spinal cord, will cause the deer to drop instantly. However he may not be dead and a second shot may be necessary. A neck shot does not always kill a deer, it may just paralyse it similar to a neck injury in humans. In this case the animal should be approached quickly and properly dispatched. If the spine is merely creased the deer may be temporarily paralysed but can recover and run off before the stalker has an opportunity of dealing adequately with the situation. If you neck-shoot a deer and it goes down but you notice any attempt to get up on the part of the deer, shoot it again immediately. In such cases the spine may not have been broken and it could quickly rise and run to cover.

A liver-shot deer will run further than an animal hit in the chest, usually running off with head down. The bleeding from such a wound is not as catastrophic and oxygenated blood can get to the brain for longer. If gut shot, the deer will usually hunch its back and kick out high in the air with its hind legs before moving for cover, sometimes slowly, with back hunched. With a stomach shot, you may hear a distinct thud as the bullet strikes the rumen. The deer will usually hunch up before heading for cover.

THE FOLLOW-UP

The deer's reaction on being hit can depend on the circumstances leading up to the shot as much as on the shot itself. If the animal has seen the stalker or been alerted to his presence, he will be vigilant and adrenalin-charged, leading to the prospect of a strong run for cover no matter how fatally wounded.

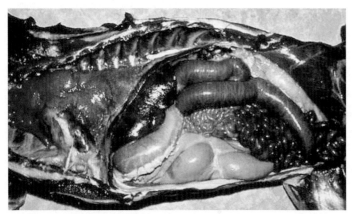

Understanding the position of organ systems within the body is essential for humane shooting and avoidance of incorrect or ineffective bullet placement

The stalker should assess the situation carefully before following up the wounded animal. He should not reveal himself if he has not already been seen, instead allowing the animal to move off at its own speed. If not panicked, a wounded deer will lie up in the nearest cover, where the stalker or his dog has a better chance of finding him.

Look for a blood trail, which will help to identify the wound and its effect and help in finding the animal. A heart and lung shot will yield a bright frothy blood trail as described above and the deer will be found dead. A liver shot deer will produce unoxygenated darker blood. The liver is very soft and purple in colour. Bits of liver tissue may be found mixed with the blood. Liver shot deer will die quite quickly but some gut shot deer can produce similar coloured blood trail so if there is little bleeding evidence about, it is safer to assume a possible gut shot and leave it a couple of hours before following up.

With a stomach wound, the blood trail may be sparse and intermittent, often with splashes of green from stomach contents. Again, give the deer time to settle down before searching and you may find that he has stiffened up or even died from the wound. If the deer is followed too quickly, it will just get up and run on further. With other wounds, the blood trail is usually of medium red colour, often with an initial abundance of blood which peters out over distance. Think about the reaction to the shot and from the evidence at the time the animal was hit, you should be able to deduce what happened. If it drops but then gets up and runs, look for bone fragments. Often with a chest shot that produces this reaction, the foreleg has been smashed below the elbow. If there is evidence of saliva, the lower jaw may have been damaged, leading to a slow death from starvation for the deer unless it is found and dispatched properly. Occasionally a deer can get a non-fatal flesh wound, particularly if shot at when head-on to the stalker. In all these situations the animal should be left for at least an hour, even up to three hours before attempting to follow up. The longer the follow-up can be delayed, the better – some experienced stalkers recommend a minimum wait of at least three hours and as long as eight hours. Practical circumstances may oblige the stalker to shorten these latter times to suit conditions.

Before starting to search for your deer, mark the point from which you took the shot. It is useful to carry a small quantity of white tissue or toilet paper for this purpose, or you can use your stalking stick to mark the spot. Mark the spot where the deer was standing when you took the shot and finally, mark the spot where he disappeared. These different points of reference will help you if you have to backtrack or as you analyse the situation. The blood trail is your best link to the deer. Always walk beside the blood trail and not directly on top if it so you don't destroy it. If you lose the blood trail, mark the last place that blood was found, then look for overturned leaves, scuff marks or broken branches that may indicate the animal's direction of travel. Deer tend to bleed more as they exert themselves, so you are more likely to find a better blood trail where the animal crossed a gully or ditch. If you still can't find the blood trail, systematically search any heavy cover that is nearby. Make every effort to retrieve a wounded animal, even if it takes all day. Above all, be patient and systematic, take your time and don't cause the deer to run from where it may be lying up.

When approaching a dead or wounded deer, do so carefully, with rifle at the ready. If thought dead, confirm this by touching the eye with a blade of grass or a twig, taking great care to avoid any possibility of being struck by an antler if only wounded. If alive but wounded, a killing shot should be administered as quickly and as safely as possible. If the deer gets up and tries to run off, shoot it anywhere in the body to get it down. The important thing in this situation is to prevent further suffering. In these circumstances a headshot may be an appropriate shot to take. Do not attempt to kill the animal with your knife.

Be aware of the fact that small, fast bullets, like those from the .22/250 (the minimum legal calibre for deer shooting in Ireland) tend to break up within the body and rarely exit from the far side of the deer. It is the exit wound, not the entry wound, which is larger and the major source of external bleeding. This is greatly reduced with the smaller, lighter calibres. The resultant reduced blood trail makes the finding of a lost animal that bit more difficult.

Obvious blood trail...

... one less obvious but with deer hair

57

CHAPTER VII

RIFLES, BALLISTICS AND ZEROING

Choosing your rifle – Ballistics (Internal, External, Terminal) - Rifle maintenance- Uunderstanding component parts – Cleaning – Mounting the ' scope - Zeroing in theory and practice.

From 1972 to 1993, deerstalkers in Ireland were limited to rifles of calibre .22. Effectively, this restriction led to widespread use of the .22/250 calibre and to a lesser extent, the 5.6 x 57 m.m. Both of these calibres satisfied the practical legal limitations and many stalkers became highly proficient in their use. Nonetheless they were (and remain) widely regarded as inadequate for the efficient and humane culling of wild deer, having regard for the species concerned and the stalking environment.

In 1993, individual legal action, stimulated by national and international opinion and best practice guidelines, led to a general loosening up of the restriction and calibres up to and including .270 are now in general use. More recently, this limitation too has been relaxed to admit calibres including .308, .30-06 and 7 m.m.

The minimum calibre as recommended by different deer organisations for use on wild deer in Ireland is .240 with a minimum bullet weight of 100 grains. Popular choices now include .243, 6.5 x 55 m. m., 6.5 x 68 m. m. and .270, with bullet weights ranging from 93 grains to 150 grains.

.22-250 Remington   *.243 Winchester*   *.270 Winchester*   *.308 Winchester*

In choosing a rifle therefore, the first decision is: what calibre? A comparative assessment of calibres and their relative performance is provided as an appendix to this manual and the individual stalker will doubtless be influenced by the practical experiences of fellow stalkers. Choice of calibre should be governed by the requirement to obtain the cleanest possible kill and in this context the fastest or heaviest round does not necessarily meet this requirement. The stalker's own physical preferences are also a consideration – the shooter should select a calibre with which he is physically comfortable, which does not produce excessive recoil proportionate to the shooter's physique and with which he can consistently place the round within the target area. No further recommendation as to calibre need be made at this stage, provided that the legal and humane requirements are met.

In any calibre, the recommended bullet structure is Cone Point, Soft Point or in certain calibres, Nosler partition, the objective being effective mushrooming of bullet head and maximum energy dispersal within the body of the shot animal. Avoid full jacket rounds, which are highly penetrative but expend little energy within the body. Availability of ammunition should be considered when selecting a rifle calibre, and once a bullet weight and type has been chosen, stick with it to ensure consistency and to avoid having to re-set sight zero with every change.

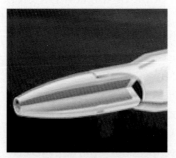

Nosler 'Vulkan'

Expansion following impact

Nosler 'Oryx' (bonded pure lead core)

Bonded core, showing expansion after impact

The Nosler Partition bullet is a bullet with two lead cores. The forward core expands easily, while the solid intermediate wall guarantees that the bullet retains more than half of the original weight for deep penetration

In comparing calibres, bullet weight and the energy of the round – the striking or killing energy (kinetic energy) of the bullet at muzzle and/or designated distances e.g. 100 yds., measured in foot-pounds, are the best yardsticks of performance in terms of killing power. The physical data of the bullet derive from the formula,

energy equals mass (weight) of bullet (measured in grams) multiplied by the squared velocity of the bullet at the point of impact, (measured in metres per second); divided by two.

Energy is therefore produced by a combination of weight and speed at point of impact. Light bullets lose velocity faster than heavy bullets, and thus energy drops faster with a light bullet than with a heavy one. Velocity is the speed with which the bullet flies through the air after leaving the barrel, measured in feet per second, at muzzle and/or at designated distances e.g. 100 or 200 yards. Velocity has little bearing on the killing power of a rifle, other than in the sense that heavy bullets are generally slower than light bullets. The bullet weight will impact on drop or trajectory over distance - the curve of the flight of the bullet through the air, between barrel and point of impact. Different calibres and different bullet weights (including weights within calibres) have different trajectories or lines of flight. The trajectory is determined by the ratio of bullet weight to powder load, also by shape and configuration of bullet.

The ideal bullet should travel at a speed sufficient to ensure as flat a trajectory as possible to minimise bullet drop at varying distances but should also be capable of sufficient penetration, mushrooming on impact without disintegrating. Ideally the bullet should be light enough to avoid any necessity of excessive powder charge, thereby reducing the recoil evident in some of the heavier calibres.

Let us briefly look at how your rifle (and in particular, the bullet fired from the rifle) actually works, in particular, considering three areas of ballistics – internal, external and terminal. Inevitably, the depth to which we can deal with this subject in this manual is limited by space, also perhaps by the reader's interest or need to know. Nonetheless, some basic knowledge is essential, and a more detailed knowledge may contribute measurably to the stalker's competence over time.

Internal ballistics concern all the aspects of the combustion phenomena occurring within the gun barrel, including pressure development and motion of the projectile along the bore of the firearm, i.e. all events until the moment the projectile exits the muzzle.

External ballistics relate to the motion of a projectile from the muzzle of a firearm to the target, i.e. the performance of the projectile during flight.

Terminal ballistics deal with the effects of projectiles on the target, i.e. the effect of the bullet when it hits the deer. .

The following illustration shows the typical structure of a bullet, before and after impact:

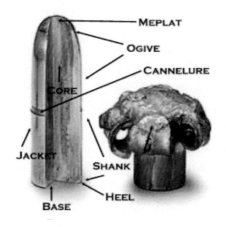

The internal process starts when you make the decision to fire your rifle. As it happens, the time lapse between decision to fire, and release of the trigger, is probably the longest time span within the process – usually about one-fifth of a second.

The firing pin travels forward, hits the primer and forces the cartridge forward into the chamber. The primer itself is pushed forward and bottoms in the primer pocket, where the priming compound is squashed against the anvil and ignited by the internal friction. The anvil is the internal part of a Boxer primer. The anvil is raised in the centre to form a cone, and has three legs which rest against the bottom of the primer pocket, spanning the flash hole. It offers concentrated resistance to the firing pin as it dents the primer, crushing the priming compound between them, which is ignited by the resulting sharp friction. The burning primer compound is thrown forward into the powder (or propellant), which ignites and starts to produce gases. These gases expand quickly, exerting pressure on the walls of the case and on the base of the bullet. The case expands to fill the chamber, the bullet is released from the neck of the case and starts its journey down the barrel, pushing the case back against the bolt face. The time taken for these various stages is still less than 0.001 of a second.

Maximum pressure within the barrel is reached in something less than 0.0005 of a second, during which time the bullet has completed about one-fifth of its journey down the barrel, achieving about one-quarter of its muzzle velocity. During this time, the bullet is rotating at up to 3,000 revolutions per second, depending on bullet type, powder load etc. Having left the barrel, the bullet will reach a target one hundred yards away in about 0.15 of a second.

The entire process therefore, from decision to bullet strike, takes less than half a second.

Numerous factors can impact on internal ballistics during this complex but speedy exercise. These include:

- Barrel length
- Bore diameter and rifling twist
  (an inadequate spin rate will lead to an unstable bullet)
- Chamber dimensions
- Bullet type – essentially, the greater the resistance met by the bullet
  inside the barrel, the higher the pressure
- Case capacity
- Primer quality and type
- The powder – including burning speed, loading density and temperature

A number of factors affect external ballistics. These include:

- Gravity
- Air resistance
- Air temperature, barometric pressure and altitude
- Bullet weight and shape
- Bullet velocity
- Wind
- Uphill or downhill influences

The degree to which these influences impact on the bullet's performance having left the barrel but before hitting the target, will vary. The effect of gravity for example, is best illustrated by understanding the trajectory of the bullet - the path of a bullet in flight. As gravity works on a bullet from the moment it exits from the muzzle, the bullet is constantly falling below the line of bore, and hence its trajectory is always curved. Rifle sights are mounted so that when the line of sight is horizontal, the bore is pointing slightly upwards - the bullet's path rises to cross the line of sight a few metres from the muzzle. However, gravity ensures that it falls to cross the line of sight a second time, much further away. By adjusting the sights, this second crossing can be made to occur at the distance of your choice, hence we say the rifle/scope/load combination is "sighted in" or "zeroed" at that distance.

Air resistance itself impacts on trajectory, by causing a drag on the bullet, causing the drooping curve described as trajectory.

Outline

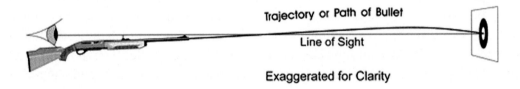

Detail

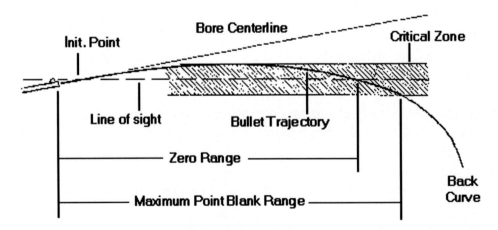

The bore's angle in relation to the line of sight is exaggerated in this drawing for purposes of clarity

Air temperature, barometric pressure and altitude all affect the density of the air – the denser the air, the greater the air resistance or drag. A rifle zeroed at sea level will have a different performance when fired over long distances at high altitude.

Bullet weight and shape, although having only a limited impact on internal ballistics, have a greater role in both external and terminal ballistics. A key characteristic is the bullet's ballistic coefficient - a mathematical factor representing the ratio of the sectional density of a bullet to its coefficient of form. Simply put, the ballistic coefficient expresses a bullet's length (relative to diameter) and aerodynamic shape, thus indicating its ability to overcome air resistance in flight. The higher its coefficient factor, the better a bullet retains its velocity and energy, and the flatter its trajectory. Most bullets have coefficients between .100 and .700. Higher coefficients are required for long-range shooting. The sectional density of the bullet is a mathematical factor expressing the ratio of a bullet's mass (weight) to its cross sectional area. Sectional density relates a bullet's diameter to its length (in a given calibre, the heavier a bullet is, the longer it is). All other factors being equal, bullets that are longer in relation to their diameter retain their velocity better, hence have flatter trajectories, hit with higher energy, and penetrate deeper, than bullets that are short relative to their diameter. Sectional density does not take into account the aerodynamic shape of a bullet, which also influences velocity retention, trajectory, etc.

Velocity, the speed of the bullet, impacts on trajectory insofar as the faster a bullet is travelling the flatter is its trajectory (although a heavier slow-moving bullet is not necessarily slowed proportionately, due to the effect of air resistance or drag). Velocity is measured in feet per second (FPS).

Wind can have a significant effect on external ballistics. Although crosswinds are more significant, a headwind (bullet fired into an oncoming wind) or tailwind (wind following bullet direction) can both cause vertical deflection. A headwind will cause the bullet to strike lower than targeted, while a tailwind will lift the bullet, causing a higher strike. In both cases, with most deer calibres and bullet weights, the effect may be marginal and can usually be measured in fractions of an inch at standard ranges.

However a crosswind of the same strength and force as that tailwind or headwind can cause a horizontal deflection of several inches, more than enough to cause an otherwise safe or fatal shot to become unsafe or merely severely wounding, or even a complete miss, despite the fact that the rifle, 'scope and shooter are otherwise correctly zeroed and accurate.

Finally, if the shot is taken uphill or downhill, especially at a steep angle, the shooter will need to compensate for the fact that in both cases, the bullet strike will be high on the target. The degree of compensation will depend on the degree of angle.

Shooting uphill – simplified illustration

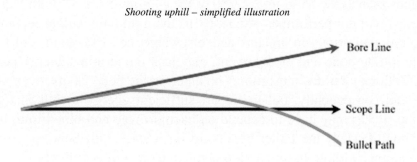

63

The reason why the bullet always shoots high for uphill and downhill shooting is based on the projectile's path in relation to the pull of gravity. Gravity works perpendicular to the horizontal line. It is the horizontal distance travelled by the bullet that is important rather than the actual linear distance travelled. A target 'scoped at 200 metres may be only 175 metres from the shooter on the horizontal plane, depending on the degree of slant. If our crosshairs are on target while aiming on a slant (uphill or downhill), bullet strike may be several inches higher than point of aim through the 'scope. It is important to recognise this possibility in the field, should it arise.

Shooting uphill – exaggerated angle of fire

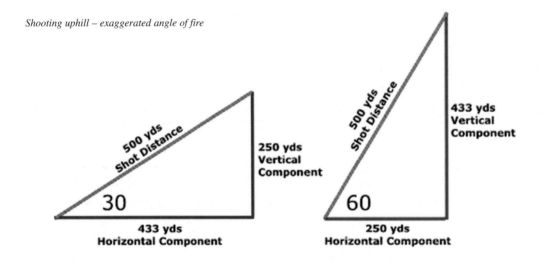

Terminal ballistics are important because they incorporate the end result of the shot – the effect of the bullet on the deer. The principal factors affecting terminal ballistics are:

- Bullet weight and type
- Bullet energy at point of impact

We need to use a round which will firstly, penetrate the body cavity efficiently; secondly, expand rapidly, ideally without exiting; and thirdly, expend as much of its remaining kinetic power or energy as possible, killing by generating hydrostatic shock waves causing tissue damage, leading to haemorrhage and death. In this context, point of aim and actual area of bullet strike are relevant. Will the bullet hit bone, as it might even with a clear broadside-on heart and lung shot, depending on shoulder placement of the deer? Bullet performance on bone will obviously be totally different than if entering body mass, composed largely of fluids.

Lighter rounds such as the 55-grain .22-250 or the 74 grain 5.6 x 57 (both legal in Ireland for all species) will not perform as efficiently as the minimum calibre recommended by various deer organisations in Ireland and elsewhere i.e. 100 grain, .240. Both may fragment on hitting bone and in any event, may lack the terminal energy needed to kill efficiently. Both may fail to "mushroom" on entering the body cavity, even assuming no deflection, and consequently, fail to impart sufficient energy to kill in the preferred manner – the stalker may have to depend on haemorrhage and blood trail, hopefully to find the animal dead. If the bullet breaks up on impact with bone, or merely passes through the animal without hitting a vital organ, a clean kill is unlikely.

The expansion of the bullet will depend on the thickness and hardness of the jacket – usually composed of an alloy of 95% copper and 5% zinc. As previously illustrated, the lead (or lead/antimony alloy) core sits in this cup or jacket and the jacket being wrapped over the base of the lead core, in hunting ammunition leaving only a small exposed lead point (usually described as hollow-point or soft-point bullets – unlike military rounds, in which the copper jacket is fitted around the nose of the lead core).

Thus, apart from what it hits, the rate of expansion of the bullet will depend on the thickness and hardness of the jacket, the hardness of the lead core and the velocity with which it is propelled. The stability of the bullet is imparted by the rate of spin imparted by the rifling of the barrel as the bullet travels through and from the barrel. These are factors to be considered when choosing not only the calibre to use but also the ammunition to use within the range which will be available for each calibre.

The ballistics table appended to this manual shows comparative performances for most popular rounds. Pay attention to the figures shown for energy. You will note that most rounds lose between 30% and 35% of their energy between muzzle and 200-yard target. Terminal energy (energy at point of impact) is what counts. Bear in mind that most ammunition has a "most recommended distance" (MRD) – a distance at which, in the opinion of the manufacturer, best performance can be expected. Significant bullet drop and loss of both energy and velocity usually occurs just on the outer edge of this MRD.

What calibre?

The basic recommendation is to use the heaviest calibre possible, commensurate with the species to be shot, and having regard for the stalker's own physical preferences, e.g. if for a lighter rifle with lower recoil, coupled with the ability to consistently place the bullet, shot after shot, precisely where it must go, then the smaller calibres will be adequate. If in doubt, choose a heavier calibre; remembering always that the primary purpose in selecting a calibre is to select one which will do the best possible job on the deer hunted, killing it efficiently, cleanly and humanely. In practical terms, the Irish stalker will be adequately equipped if he chooses a calibre in the range .243 to .270 or 7 m.m. (including all variations such as the 6.5 x 55 or 6.5 x 68).

140 gr. 6.5 x 55 m.m. bullet, muzzle energy 2784 foot-pounds.

.243 Winchester.   .270 Winchester.   .308 Winchester.

The Irish stalker is limited to a non-automatic bolt-action rifle, the only type permitted under Irish law. This may be single-shot or with a magazine carrying from three to five rounds.

Steyer Mannlicher Classic (Carbine)

There are many makes of rifle from which to choose, and budget will be a major consideration. Mannlicher (including Mannlicher-Steyr and Mannlicher-Schonauer) and Mauser are two excellent makes, either of which will serve the stalker a lifetime. The Sauer is a very handsome and functional modern rifle, while the Sako, Tikka and Krico can be recommended also.

Tikka T3 Hunter

Parker Hale have a name for producing a reliable if basic range of rifles, while there are various relatively new makes available from Sweden and Norway, such as the Varberger. While wooden stocks are traditional, stocks are now available in alternative and completely weather-resistant materials. The choice in this area is very much a personal one. The weight of the rifle is a big consideration for those who stalk in mountainous terrain.

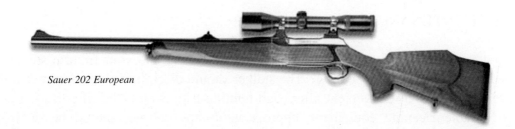

Sauer 202 European

The length of the stock and the height of the comb should be suitable for the physique of the stalker, having regard to the telescopic sight to be used. Models are available for both the right and left handed person. The pressure required to pull the trigger, measured from ounces to pounds, should also be compatible with the user's needs and skills, with many manufacturers providing what are called set-trigger arrangements – a double trigger, with one trigger used to 'set' or cock the other. In some models, a single trigger can be used to set the mechanism, with the first slight pressure, or forward pressure, setting the trigger and further pressure, or backward pressure, releasing it.

Mauser Model 66

Mauser M 03

Best advice is to try to handle a variety of firearms before choosing one. Any good firearms dealer should be able to advise further on availability and price of latest models, while the second-hand market may also produce a suitable firearm within the novice stalker's budget.

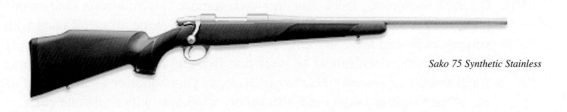

Sako 75 Synthetic Stainless

RIFLE MAINTENANCE

The first essential of rifle maintenance is regular cleaning and your firearm should be cleaned carefully after every outing. The stalker should discipline himself into cleaning his firearm as soon as convenient after each hunting trip, even if the rifle has not been fired. Suitable cleaning equipment, appropriate to the calibre, should be on hand. Equipment needed includes

- cleaning rod
- brushes and jags, of the proper size for the calibre.
  Brushes should be phosphor bronze
- solvent, for cleaning the bore
- lubricant (a fine oil such as WD40 is suitable)
- silicone-impregnated cloth
- linseed oil or equivalent, for cleaning the stock
- lens cleaning kit, including soft cloth, brush and an aerosol air spray, for use on the telescopic sight.

CLEANING YOUR RIFLE

I)   Barrel: remove any loose fouling with a solvent-soaked patch on a jag. If there is heavy fouling, use a phosphor bronze brush to remove and finish by running a clean patch through, several times if necessary, until the patch emerges completely free of fouling. Leave the bore dry unless being stored, in which case a very thin coating of lubricant can be applied (with a patch) to help prevent internal rusting.

II)   Bolt: wipe clean with a solvent-soaked cloth. As with the barrel bore, leave dry unless going into storage, in which case apply a thin coat of lubricant. Remember – for security reasons your bolt should be stored separately from the rifle. It is recommended that the bolt be stored with spring tension released i.e. not cocked.

III)   Chamber and action: use a toothbrush or if available, tools designed for the purpose, to remove any fouling, dirt or specks of brass (which can be pared off from a cartridge by the locking lugs of the action). Clean the chamber with a chamber brush or with a soft cloth on a jag. If you need to use a solvent ensure that it does not get into the trigger mechanism.

IV)   Trigger and Safety: use an aerosol air spray to remove dust or small particles of dirt. Avoid using lubricant as you may clog up the trigger mechanism.

V)   Magazine: use a dry brush and a soft cloth and leave dry, unless going into storage.

VI)   External metalwork, stock and fore-end: remove any moisture, dust, mud or blood with a soft cloth or toothbrush as necessary. Wipe all metal parts with a silicone cloth and leave dry unless being left for a time, in which case apply a light lubricant. If the timber of stock and fore-end has an oiled finish, apply a small amount of linseed oil occasionally, using your hands or a soft cloth. If they are of varnished or lacquered finish simply wipe over with a silicone cloth.

VII)   Scope and mounts: use a soft brush or aerosol air spray to remove dust and wipe over with a silicone cloth, taking care not to scratch the lenses.

THE TELESCOPIC SIGHT

The choice of telescopic sight is at least of equal importance to the stalker as selection of rifle. Certainly it is important to spend as much money as you can on the sight. If the rifle and sight are properly zeroed the stalker can guarantee that at a particular distance the bullet will always hit the exact spot that the cross hairs of the reticle indicate. Under set conditions, any deviation from this in the properly zeroed rifle is due to stalker error.

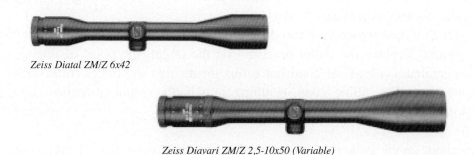

Zeiss Diatal ZM/Z 6x42

Zeiss Diavari ZM/Z 2,5-10x50 (Variable)

There are numerous types of reticle available, of which those shown here are a small selection

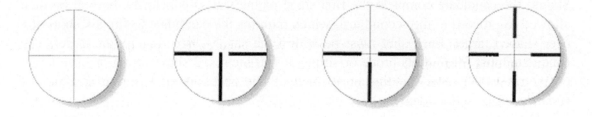

When purchasing a telescopic sight, ensure that it has good light-gathering qualities. The same principles apply as for binoculars. Most deer will be shot at dawn and dusk and with good optics they will be seen clearly in both binoculars and telescopic sight long after they are no longer visible with the naked eye. The stalker can choose between fixed and variable power sights. 6X magnification is a popular and useful all-round configuration e.g. 6 x 42. Variable power 'scopes are useful but there is usually some loss in light-gathering capability as magnification increases. Novice stalkers should opt for a fixed power 'scope or leave a variable permanently at a tried and trusted setting. The greater the magnification the greater the detectable wobble. Cheaper scopes are often not intended for use on full-bore rifles and may not hold zero, they are also more likely to fog up in wet conditions. There are a number of different reticles available, choose one that will be good in low light conditions.

Do not mount a telescopic sight too far back on the rifle as it can hit the eye on recoil.

ZEROING YOUR RIFLE

The stalker must have absolute confidence in his rifle. This means that he must be sure that, eliminating all human error and external conditions such as wind etc., his rifle is capable of placing a series of rounds exactly on the point of aim (POA). Remember that a telescopic sight does a number of things:

a) it "brings the target closer" – meaning that it magnifies the target
b) it allows the shooter to precisely fix his point of aim on the target, having regard for the distance involved
c) as it magnifies the target, so too does it magnify human error – if the 'scope is not calibrated to place the bullet precisely on the target, the point of impact will be exaggerated. Under field conditions, this means that the bullet could strike many inches from the killing zone, resulting in a badly wounded and possibly a lost animal.

It is incumbent on the stalker to ensure that his firearm is up to the job and thereafter he must practise regularly to ensure that his physical skills match the technical performance of the rifle and telescopic sight. For certification purposes under the Hunter Competence Assessment Programme, candidates will be required to satisfy the assessors in a two-stage test of shooting competence. The initial part of the test requires the candidate to place three shots in a four-inch circle at a distance of 100 metres, in the prone position. Should the candidate complete the first stage of the test satisfactorily, he will be then allowed to proceed to the second test, which requires the candidate to fire six shots at a deer shaped target. Each shot must be within the seven-score ring on the target. The candidate must fire 2 shots prone or sitting at 100 metres, 2 shots sitting or kneeling at 60 metres and 2 shots standing at 40 metres. The necessity of ensuring accuracy of firearm will be self-evident.

PRACTICAL REQUIREMENTS WHEN ZEROING

Remember, the primary objective is to ensure accuracy of rifle and telescopic sight. Zeroing is not intended to be a test of the shooter's own physical competence. Consequently, it is perfectly acceptable to use a bench rest and vice, or at the very least, to ensure that the rifle and 'scope are well supported, perhaps rested on sandbags to ensure maximum stability (if not in a vice).

The following are needed when zeroing your rifle:

a) a safe place – either an authorised rifle range or somewhere with a substantial backstop, preferably sheltered from the wind
b) rifle and properly mounted telescopic sight, both in maximum serviceable condition
c) supply of ammunition, all of the same batch, all bullets of the same type and weight
d) targets – minimum four inch bull's-eye, with minimum eight inches of white space all around
e) target holder and materials with which to fix the paper targets

f) bench rest with vice or rest (e.g. table with sandbags). If not using a bench rest or equivalent, then zeroing is best done in the prone position

g) spotting 'scope, if available – it will eliminate much walking to and from the target

h) pencil and paper

i) ear protectors

j) optical bore-sighter, if you have one. A bore-sighter will save ammunition and repay its initial cost over time

k) ruler or tape measure, for measuring the bullet group.

There is no point in zeroing your rifle unless weather conditions are suitable. This means a wind-free day, with good light. Variations in light will lead to variations in performance.

READY TO ZERO

Normally, not more than six to eight inches of adjustment are required for zeroing. In extreme cases, ten to twelve inches are needed. We suggest you carefully check your mounting system first. Your sight is optically centred from the factory, which means the erector system in your 'scope sits right in the middle of the tube. Any adjustments made using the W/E dials will move the erector system from the centre. Make sure that you can zero the Point of Impact (bullet impact point) and Point of Aim (crosshair point) without using excessive amount of W/E adjustment.

FOR THOSE WHO DO NOT HAVE AN OPTICAL BORE-SIGHTER

Mount the sight on your rifle and tighten all screws. Set the target at 25 yards. From bench rest, aim at the centre of your target and shoot 2 or 3 rounds. Examine your target, check how far your Point of Impact (POI) is from your Point of Aim (POA). If the bullet hits were more than 3 inches (12 inches/100 yards) apart from where you aimed at, you have problem(s) with your mounting system. Do not use W/E adjustment screw. Adjust the mounting system first.

FOR THOSE WHO ARE USING AN OPTICAL BORE-SIGHTER

With the top portion of your mounting rings open, put your riflescope on your rings, determine how far the centre of your crosshairs is from the centre of your bore-sighter grid. If they are more than 3 squares (12 inches/100 yards) apart from each other, you have problem(s) with your mounting system. Do not use W/E adjustment screw. Adjust the mounting system first.

Bushnell Magnetic Optical Bore Sight

NOTE: Never force the W/E screws past their natural stop. Internal damage can result, rendering the 'scope inoperative. The most common occurrence with "over-adjusting" includes: power change system jamming, broken inner lenses, poor image quality, insufficient grouping of shots, and limited or irregular movement of POI alignment.

AFTER YOU HAVE BORE SIGHTED AND IT IS CLOSE TO ZERO

Locate a safe place to test fire and fine-tune your weapon, preferable a firing range. The next step is to find a stable surface from which to fire. If you cannot hold the weapon still, it will not zero in correctly. A couple of small sandbags will come in handy for stabilizing the weapon. A dry patch should be run through the bore to remove any oil. With a target set up at 100 yards you are now ready to test fire. Holding the crosshairs steady on the target, squeeze off a round. Repeat this two more times to get a three shot group. Retrieve your target and triangulate the shots to get an average point of impact. Measure from that POI to the bull's eye where you aimed. This measurement can now be adjusted with adjusting screws located under the top and side (screw-off caps) located in the centre of the 'scope. The arrows on the dial show which direction they will move the bullet. Turn the adjusting screws according to the MOA (Minute of Angle) scale on the dial. If they say 1/4 MOA, that means one click will move the bullet 1/4" at 100 yards. Note, if you zero at a different yardage, say 50 yards, one click will move the bullet only 1/8" at 50 yards. Once you have adjusted the windage (side screw) and the elevation (top screw), you are now ready for another 3 shot group. Repeat this process until you are satisfied with the results. It is important to allow the barrel to cool down in between the three-shot groups as heating of the barrel can cause bullet flight to vary. It is also recommended to swab the bore between shots with a dry patch to reduce build-up. Do not use any cleaning fluid or oil on the swab as this can affect bullet flight. For deer hunting, it is suggested that you may want to adjust the elevation an inch or two above bull's-eye at 100 yards. This will give your weapon extended range and still keep you in the kill zone at 100 yards and less. However, you must have regard for the intricacies of bullet performance – including velocity, energy and bullet drop – as dealt with earlier in this chapter and detailed in the appendix on ballistics. Keep your ambitions within the range of your competence – do not attempt to match the manufacturer's "most recommended distance" for the ammunition used unless you can achieve consistent accuracy and performance at a lesser range. With modern rounds, the MRD is often 200 yards or more, even for the smaller calibres. However 200-plus yards is at the outer edge of recommended distance for deer hunting, and outside the range of competence of many stalkers when it comes to consistently hitting the killing zone.

Sighting-in should be done on a windless day or at least on a day when the wind is 5 m.p.h. or less. Before using the rifle in the field, make sure to run a dry patch through the bore to remove any lubricant used after the last cleaning.

REMEMBER:

- Treat your weapon as being loaded at all times.
- Communicate your intentions with others on the range.
- Check down-range every time before firing.
- Take along hearing and eye protection.
- Don't forget the targets!

PROBLEMS

Problems zeroing may be attributable to two sources – either the equipment or the shooter.

a)   The equipment

Check the following:

I)   Is the telescopic sight properly mounted? Is it secure, with all screws tight? Is there any movement between rifle and 'scope?

II)   Ammunition – is all ammunition fresh, dry and of the same type, same batch and same weight?

III)   Is the barrel properly bedded – no warping arising from moisture and if a floating barrel, fully freely floating?

IV)   Is the action properly bedded – are all screws tight?

V)   Is the barrel clean, free of fouling, solvents or lubricants?

VI)   Is the barrel cool? A hot barrel will cause wild shots. Take your time between groups

VII)   Is the 'scope itself undamaged?

b)   The shooter

I)   Are you holding the rifle properly? Make sure your grip is positive and your stance comfortable. Eliminate barrel cant (cant error is the result of not holding the rifle bore axis and the 'scope axis in a vertical plane)

II)   Is parallax interfering with your vision? Parallax leads to a distorted view of an object viewed through rifle sights, due to position of viewer in relation to sights and/or object viewed. Most 'scopes are parallax-free at 100 metres but the human eye can be subject to it at any distance. For a simple understanding of how parallax affects your sighting plane, hold out a pencil at arm's length so that it covers your view of a more distant object. Now close each eye in turn. The pencil seems to move relative to the distant object when a different eye is closed. Each eye looks at the pencil from a slightly different direction. With both eyes open you get more visual clues as to how far away any object is. Your brain instinctively determines the object's distance from the slight change in direction (measured by the angle - P). This method of measuring distances is called parallax

III)   Are you anticipating recoil, leading to flinching?

IV)   Are you pulling the trigger, instead of gently squeezing it? A pull, especially if anticipating recoil, will inevitably lead to flinching

V)   Are you fatigued? If you haven't achieved your desired grouping results after three or four groups, you are unlikely to achieve them in the session. Come back another day.

VI)   Is the weather on your side – no wind, rain, excessive sunshine or extreme of heat or cold? If the weather is against you, don't fight it, come back another day.

CHAPTER VIII

FIREARMS SAFETY

Common reasons why accidents occur (in and around vehicles, loading and unloading, negotiating obstacles, crawling or stalking with loaded rifle) - Barrel obstruction - Storage of weapons (recommended security provisions at home and in transport) - Weapon proficiency - Steady shooting positions - Background to shot - Non-firearm risks (knives, weather, dragging) – Insurance - Health and Safety Agency

Safety, inside and outside the home, should be the top priority of every firearms user.

Safety in the home is achieved by careful handling and by safe, secure storage. Safety outside the home is achieved by being aware of the many circumstances that can lead to accident or injury and by talking steps to avoid them.

Carelessness and ignorance are the most common causes of accidents and both can be avoided if not eliminated.

SAFETY IN THE HOME

Although there is currently no legal requirement on the firearms owner to install a gun cabinet or gun safe, impending legislation (section 30, Criminal Justice Bill, 2004 – amendment of section 4 of the Firearms Act, 1925) may shortly alter this situation and meanwhile it is strongly recommended that every user do so. There is a wide range of options available in Ireland today and any good firearms dealer will stock examples. Be sure that the model chosen carries a British or Irish standards kite mark.

Expect to spend up to €200 for a basic model, and more as you progress up the scale of full security.

Safes should be bolted to wall and floor and have a prise-resistant door, preferably with two five-lever mortice locks or equivalent. Chose a location in the home which is unobtrusive and not apparent to the opportunistic intruder.

Rifle, firing bolt and ammunition should ideally be stored separately.

If there are children (or inquisitive adults) in the house, the need for security is absolutely paramount. Every opportunity should be taken to instil a sense of safety in younger persons, who will naturally be curious where firearms are concerned. The rule should be that anybody picking up a firearm, for any purpose, should first and foremost ensure that it is not loaded or cocked. Firearms should never be pointed at any person or any living thing by way of a practical joke or threat. Remember, misuse of firearms may lead to revocation of firearms certificate.

When cleaning your firearm, start by ensuring that the chamber and magazine are both empty. Never assume that they are, always assume that they might be loaded (and all too often are, having been stored carelessly or in a hurry).

SAFETY OUTSIDE THE HOME

Your firearm should always be transported with ammunition and firing bolt removed. It should be safe and secure against accidental damage and against opportunistic theft. A

Gun safes come in a variety of shapes, sizes, configurations and price levels

rifle slip is the minimum protection and ideally, some form of secure container should be incorporated in the boot of your vehicle, out of sight. Remember, "out of sight" in this context does not mean "out of mind", it means "out of danger".

There are a number of specific occasions of danger against which the firearms user should guard at all times. These include situations that may arise:

- in and around vehicles

- loading and unloading the firearm

- when negotiating obstacles such as fences and ditches

- when crawling or stalking with rifle loaded

- when there is a danger of a barrel obstruction such as mud or snow

- when there is no adequate backstop for the shot to be taken.

Most deer hunters will drive to their stalking ground, hopefully with firearm safe and secure in the boot of the car.

The Garda Siochana recommend and advise against identifying your vehicle as likely to contain a firearm by carrying a sticker on the windscreen or elsewhere on the vehicle indicating membership of a gun club.

On arriving at the ground, the tendency is to immediately load and cock the rifle, especially if stalking in forestry, when the unexpected is often the rule and a deer can appear at short notice and close range from behind the nearest tree. This is a dangerous

FIREARMS IN USE

Prescribed format for warning sign, to be posted at all Coillte forest property entrances when shooting. Minimum size 400 m.m. x 600 m.m.

tendency and the hunter should remind himself (and any companions) from the outset of the need to maintain best practice in terms of safety at all times.

The hunter may load his rifle on arrival at the stalking ground but the first round should be unchambered and the rifle carried, slung or unslung, with the bolt closed in place over the bullet and the safety catch on. It is the work of only a split second to slide the safety off and chamber a round, ready to fire, as and when a deer appears. If in company with other stalkers, the rifle should be carried unloaded and with bolt open. Better a deer lost than a stalker lost.

Remember, it is a condition of the Coillte Teoranta forest licence that signs must be posted at all forest access points when hunting deer on Coillte property. These must be in the prescribed form.

Be especially alert and careful when loading or unloading the firearm as in these circumstances, you are dealing with live rounds of ammunition and, usually, with firing bolt in place in the receiver of the firearm. Undo the safety catch, slide back the bolt and remove the ammunition or magazine with barrel held deliberately in the air. When you are sure that all live ammunition has been removed, either remove the firing bolt, or close it and make the firing mechanism safe. If in company, make a point of showing others that the firearm is safe.

When negotiating obstacles such as fences or ditches, the rifle should be made safe by unloading it before attempting to get over the obstacle. The rifle should be put down on the ground while dealing with the obstacle, rather than held aloft or leant against a fencepost, wire or bush. Once over the obstacle, check that no foreign matter such as mud, grass or a twig has entered the muzzle of the rifle. It is useful to carry a pull-through for this purpose.

Once your quarry has been sighted or if you are scouting terrain where deer are likely to be found, you may find yourself crawling through bracken or gorse. You can do this with your rifle slung across your back, or held across your chest as you inch your way forward. In either case, it is vital that your firearm is in safe mode and that you avoid snagging it or any twig or other obstacle. If in company with others, it is equally vital that you know where your companions are. Your objective is to be unseen and hopefully unscented by any deer in the vicinity but your position should be known to your companions, and theirs to you. Good communication is essential and a game plan should be worked out and agreed in advance.

As when negotiating obstacles, barrel obstruction can easily occur, unknown to you. It is essential to check for any obstruction after your crawl through bracken, gorse or heather.

A solid backstop is essential when gauging whether the shot is safe to take. Never shoot into or towards the skyline. It is not sufficient that you see nothing behind your target – there must be an adequate background to prevent the bullet carrying on into the unknown, either following a miss or having passed through the animal's body without fragmentation. It is not unknown for a bullet to travel up to a mile after discharge, and still possessing enough terminal energy to cause death or serious injury. Watch out for the possibility of ricochet in the event of a miss – a ricochet can occur against almost any surface, including water.

When considering the safety of a shot one must also consider other deer in the vicinity of the animal being culled. Very often a hind will be obscuring her calf, and what might be a perfect fatal shot to her can cause a non-fatal injury to the calf.

When hunting in forestry, remember that it is a condition of the Coillte forest licence that no shots are taken along or across forest rides or forest roads.

STEADY SHOOTING POSITIONS

From the point of view of personal safety as well as from that of ensuring maximum accuracy of shot, it is essential to adopt a safe and steady shooting position.

Once your target has been identified, and assuming your quarry has not yet seen or scented you, you should adopt a shooting position best suited to the circumstances.

Possibilities include:

- prone, rested
- kneeling, rested
- sitting, rested
- standing, rested
- standing, off-hand (unrested).

Sitting, rested position

Offhand, standing position

Kneeling position

Prone position

Of all of these, the last is the least desirable. In all cases, you should ensure a clear line of fire and a safe and adequate backstop. The slightest obstacle may deflect your bullet, particularly with the lower and lighter calibres. A branch, a twig, a small rock, even a blade of grass can all impact on the accuracy and the safety of the shot. Remember, a clear picture through the lens of the telescopic sight is no guarantee that the muzzle of the rifle is unobstructed – so check and double-check every time.

For most stalkers, the prone rested shot is likely to be the safest and most accurate. Ensure that the rifle is rested on a suitable and stable surface and avoid scratching of timber fore-end or stock.

The kneeling rested shot can be equally safe and stable, with the elbow of the supporting arm rested on the opposing knee.

The sitting rested shot, usually with legs crossed and providing a stable rest, is another option.

All of the above positions can be made extremely steady with use of a bipod or tripod with extendable legs,

The standing rested shot, with rifle fore-end supported by a stalking stick of adequate height and best configuration (the thumbstick), perhaps stuck in the ground and further stabilised by a "snooker cue" grip, can often offer adequate stability and consequently, safety. The optimum height or length of stalking stick is one on which the "vee" of the thumb grip is of parallel height to the stalker's eye-line. A rough rule of thumb suggests that if the stalker is five feet ten inches in height, the stick too should be five feet ten inches long. It is easier to position the stick at an angle, provided it is stable, than for the stalker to crouch down because the stick is too short.

If the standing unrested shot is the only shot available to the stalker, it is incumbent on the stalker to ensure that he is fully capable of placing the bullet properly, also to ensure that the shot is truly safe, not merely instinctive or opportunistic. Full use should be made of the rifle sling, in the manner illustrated. Failing use of sling, the various stances adopted by competitive rifle shots can be considered, but from the point of view of safety in a shooting environment which may not be as controlled as the rifle range, are not recommended.

Prone position

Sitting/kneeling, rested

Firearms safety is best achieved by regular handling and practice. Take full use of every opportunity to practice the various shooting positions and to fully understand the performance of your rifle and ammunition. Remember to use adequate protection whenever appropriate, especially on the rifle range. This means adequate protection for eyes and ears.

Non-firearm risks can arise. These include risks arising from improper use of knives, inadequate preparation against changing weather conditions, the danger of a fall in the field or even the danger of injury when dragging a deer following a successful shot. Common sense will reduce or eliminate likelihood of injury or worse from these sources but the risk will always be present. Remember, hunter firearms competence will be assessed partially on shooting accuracy but the safety element will be of paramount importance and stalkers seeking to be certified as competent with their firearm will require to satisfy examiners by oral examination and physical demonstration as well as by accuracy on the range.

To summarise, the safe firearms user should observe the following key rules at all time:

- Firearms should be stored securely and unloaded when not actually in use and they should be inaccessible to unauthorised users at all times. Especially, always store your firearm safely away from children
- Learn the mechanical and handling characteristics of your firearm thoroughly before attempting to use it in the field
- Be sure the gun itself is safe to use, completely without mechanical defect, before attempting to use it
- Clean your gun regularly and make absolutely sure it is unloaded before attempting to clean it
- Do not rely solely on the safety catch of your firearm
- Treat every gun as if it loaded. The only "safe" gun is the one you have checked personally - and then checked again
- Use the correct ammunition for the firearm in question
- Don't carry out significant repairs or attempt even legal modifications unless you are truly competent. Have it serviced regularly by someone who is competent
- In the field, be sure of your target and of what lies beyond it
- Always keep the muzzle of the firearm pointed in a safe direction. Never, ever point your gun at another person, even in jest
- Be sure the barrel is clear of any obstruction before firing
- If your rifle fails to fire when the trigger is pulled, handle with great care
- In company, always assume that every other firearm is loaded and therefore a source of danger. Make sure your companions follow the same safety rules you do and don't be afraid to pull them up if they don't. Pass or accept only open and unloaded guns
- Accuracy supports safety. Accuracy is attained only by regular practice
- Take utmost care to correctly identify and assess your proposed target. Double-check, then treble-check. This is especially important in conditions of low light
- Make absolutely sure you have a totally safe and adequate backstop. The bullet from your rifle can travel extreme distances and still be capable of killing
- Remember, alcohol and guns are a deadly combination. Never consume anything that would even mildly impair your judgment or physical coordination when you're using a firearm.

There are a number of specific terms and conditions attached to the Coillte Teoranta licence to hunt deer on Coillte forest property, with which all nominated stalkers should be aware. These are set out below; other conditions may be attached to the individual licence agreement between Collite as licensor, and the licensee. A specimen Sporting Licence is appended to this manual and is intended as a general reference and guide only. All Coillte forest properties on which deer hunting licences are granted are subject to Hazard Identification and Risk Assessment (HIRA) and licensees are required to acknowledge recognition and awareness of all known hazards and risks on individual licensed areas. Licensees should ensure that all nominated stalkers are also fully aware of all known hazards and risks, in addition to the safety protocols noted above. The prudent stalker will also carry out his own hazard identification and risk assessment on other land on which deer culling is carried out, before exercising rights on private (non-Coillte) land.

A NOTE ON INSURANCE

Despite all safeguards, accidents can and do happen. In this context, it is foolhardy to stalk deer (or indeed, pursue almost any outdoor activity) without some level of insurance cover or compensation plan, taking in injury or death of a third party or the policy holder, damage to property including livestock and bloodstock, as well as loss, theft or damage to firearm or other equipment e.g. binoculars, camera etc.

It is a strict condition of hunting on Coillte forest property as licensee or nominated stalker that insurance cover of not less than €2.5MN. be carried by those exercising rights under the terms of the Coillte licence and Coillte will not normally issue their shooting permit in respect of the forest property under licence without proof of cover, valid for the season under licence.

Coillte accept the NARGC Hunting Compensation Scheme as the equivalent of ordinary insurance cover. This is administered through the network of NARGC affiliated gun clubs and game associations nationally.

Members of the Irish Timber Growers' Association also require that persons hunting deer on land owned by any member of that association be adequately covered by insurance and may also seek an indemnification of the land owner in respect of any claims or damage arising from the hunting on wild deer, whereby the landowner is "held harmless" in respect of any claim.

In fact, most private landowners will require persons exercising rights as visitors or recreational users to demonstrate insurance cover, notwithstanding the provisions of the Occupiers' Liability Act, 1995 (*q.v.*).

Most insurance providers will provide cover under the terms of ordinary householder insurance policies, subject to assessment of risk and possibly to payment of additional premium.

As indicated above, the NARGC Compensation Fund provides adequate and acceptable cover, as does cover provided to members of the Countryside Alliance (Ireland) and IFA Countryside.

SPECIFIC TERMS AND CONDITIONS OF THE COILLTE TEORANTA LICENCE TO HUNT DEER ON COILLTE FOREST PROPERTY, WITH WHICH LICENSEES AND NOMINATED STALKERS MUST COMPLY

- To post notices in the format approved by the licensor at all entrances to the lands prior to commencement of stalking and to remove same on cessation of stalking
- Not to exercise rights along any forest roads, public pathways or in the vicinity of any residence or buildings
- To exercise the rights of stalking and culling deer in a proper and sportsmanlike manner and in accordance with all current wildlife legislation
- Not to cause nuisance to, annoyance or damage to the licensor's property, stock, fences, gates or any other property or interfere in any way with the licensor's undertaking on or use of the lands or disturb, damage or interfere with or move any of the flora, fauna, wildlife, game (other than deer) or other natural phenomena on the lands
- To keep the lands clean, tidy and in good order and to pay for any damage thereto or expense of clearing the same caused by any damage
- Not to light fires on the land
- To close all gates and take such reasonable steps as may be necessary to protect the lands
- Not to duplicate any keys issued by the licensor and to return such keys on the termination/expiration of the licence
- Not to dispose of any viscera or other carcass waste on the lands
- To notify the relevant authorities of any abnormal conditions or suspected diseases observed in the culled animals
- The Coillte licence is granted solely for the purpose of stalking and culling wild deer and the rights hereunder shall be exercised only during the declared shooting season as determined under current wildlife legislation and only during the hours between dawn and 11 am
- On application, written permission may be granted by the licensor to the licensee to allow evening shooting for the period of two hours before dusk. Such permission shall only be in respect of specifically approved sites and shall be restricted to shooting from "high seats" or similar elevated shooting positions only. The licensee shall however indemnify and save harmless the licensor from and against all actions arising out of injury to any person or loss or damage to any property whatsoever resulting from or in any way connected with or arising from the use of such "high seats".
- All persons intending to hunt deer on Coillte's property must have access to a trained tracking dog for the recovery and humane dispatch of any deer injured from shooting

(Season 2004-2005)

CHAPTER IX

DEER HUNTING AND THE LAW

Wildlife Act, 1976 – Wildlife (Amendment) Act, 2000 – Firearms Acts, 1925 to 2000 – Control of Dogs Act, 1986 – Occupiers' Liability Act, 1995

Persons hunting wild deer in Ireland require to be conversant with various pieces of legislation, including those relating to protection of wild deer and to firearms. This legislation includes the Wildlife Acts, 1976 to 2000 and the Firearms Acts, 1925 to 2000. Other legislation affecting the hunter may include Control of Dogs Act, 1986 and in certain circumstances, the Occupiers' Liability Act, 1995.

Wild deer in the Republic of Ireland are protected by the Wildlife Act, 1976 (as amended), and in Northern Ireland by the Wildlife (Northern Ireland) Order, 1985.

Deer legislation varies as between the Republic of Ireland and Northern Ireland (see below)

The Wildlife Act, 1976, Number 39 of 1976, became law on December 22nd 1976 and was brought into operation by Ministerial Order on June 1st 1977. The Act was amended by the Wildlife (Amendment) Act, 2000 (Number 38 of 2000), Section 3 and 46 of which were enacted by Statutory Instrument No. 71 of 2001 of 2001 and all other Sections (except Section 36) by Statutory Instrument No 371 of 2001.

Its principal objective is the conservation of wildlife and the protection of certain flora and fauna, and in its nature it is an enabling Act, with sufficient powers granted to the Minister responsible to introduce supplementary regulations to meet needs as time or situations demand.

The 1976 Act introduced Open and Closed Seasons for the hunting of wild deer, and a system of annual licensing for deer hunters. Open Seasons may be suspended for up to two months for any specified reason. Deer may be hunted with staghounds under licence, irrespective of any Closed Season. The Act also provides for the killing of deer in the Closed Season, and sets out terms on which deer can be hunted, captured or killed for purposes of scientific research; and also covers the sale of venison to hotels, restaurants and private individuals. The laws of trespass are extended to cover trespass specifically in pursuit of deer. A notable feature of the Act is that in certain situations the onus of proof of innocence (such as authority to be on land in pursuit of deer) lies with a defendant, rather than it falling on the prosecution to prove guilt, which can be deemed assumed (such as in trespass, armed or otherwise).

The following items are matters relating to wild deer, covered by specific provisions of the Wildlife Act, 1976 (section references are to sections of the Principal Act except where otherwise stated):

- **DEFINITION OF "HUNTING"**: the word "hunt" is formally defined; it means to "stalk, pursue, chase, drive, flush, capture, course, attract, follow, search for, lie in wait for, take, trap or shoot by any means whether with or without dogs, and includes killing in the course of hunting"; section 2. As amended by section 6 (2) of the Wildlife (Amendment) Act, 2000, hunting includes killing in the course of hunting. Although the pursuit of the activities contained in the original definition of "hunt" (above) in connection with photography, painting or sketching was specifically excluded in section 2 of the Wildlife Act, 1976, that exclusion is removed by amendment of the definition by section 6 (1) (j) of the Wildlife (Amendment) Act, 2000. Note also that section 31 of the Wildlife (Amendment) Act, 2000 amends section 23 of the Principal Act and provides protection for the resting and breeding places of wild deer; it also provides that "the Minister may grant a licence to a person to take or make photographic, video or other pictures of a protected wild animal of a species so specified on or near the breeding place of such an animal", thus suggesting that it is an offence to so act without a licence.

- **SHOOTING OF WILD DEER:** The Minister may make an order permitting open season hunting of (otherwise protected) specified game animals, either throughout the State or in specified areas. In practice, the only species likely to be involved are hares and deer; section 25 (1). An order may specify the method of hunting (e.g. by shooting, coursing etc.) and, as in the case of game birds, may impose a limit on the number which may be killed by individuals; section 25 (2). The Minister may suspend an open season for up to two months for any specified reason (e.g. disease, severe weather conditions etc.). The suspension can apply to the country as a whole or to a particular area or areas and may relate to any species; section 27). section 23 (5) makes it an offence to hunt except under licence or permission from the Minister, or to injure a deer except when hunting under licence or permission, or to wilfully interfere with the breeding places of wild deer. This last offence could be invoked in the case of burning of heather, for example for the benefit of grouse, although section 23 (7) (a) removes the offence if committed while legitimately engaged in agriculture, forestry, zoology or other scientific pursuit.

- **INJURED OR DISABLED DEER:** may be captured in order to kill them or it humanely, or in order to care for them or it, intending to release them or it later; section 23 (7), (d) & (e).

- **ACCIDENTAL KILLING OR INJURY:** for example by running over a deer while lawfully driving a motor car, is not an offence; section 23 (7) (iv).

- **EXCEPTIONS UNDER LICENCE:** the Minister may grant a licence to capture and/or humanely kill any deer for an educational, scientific or other purpose specified in the licence (in closed or open Season); section 23 (6).

- **QUALIFIED PERSONS:** a person may not hunt or kill wild deer with firearms on any land except during an open season and in accordance with an appropriate hunting licence. He or she must also be at least sixteen years of age, and be entitled to sporting rights over the land (or be the guest, servant or agent, or have the written permission of someone entitled to sporting rights over the land; or be a member of a group entitled to sporting rights over the land; or be someone whom the Minister has declared qualified); section 28. Note: section 28 of the Principal Act is amended by section 37 of the Wildlife (Amendment) Act, 2000, which provides that the Minister may require an applicant for a deer hunting licence to supply satisfactory evidence that the applicant is a competent person to hold such a licence e.g. by having achieved the standards imposed by any hunter competence training and assessment programme which itself meets required standards. A person may be disqualified from holding a deer hunting licence on conviction for any offence under the Act; section 75 (1) (see below under Penalties).

- **LICENCES:** may be issued (by the Minister, through the National Parks & Wildlife Service) either to a person ordinarily resident in the State to hunt deer; section 29 (1); or to a person ordinarily resident outside the State to hunt both game birds or game animals; section 29 (2). Residents and non-residents are both issued with the same form of deer hunting licence. Note: an applicant is not required to be in prior possession of a firearms certificate in order to obtain a deer hunting licence. Applicants are however required to give the calibre, bullet weight, maker's name and identifying number of the firearm intended to be used. There is no provision in the Act for a charge to be levied in respect of issue of a hunting licence. However section 29 is amended by section 4 of the Firearms (Firearms Certificates for Non-Residents) Act, 2000, which provides that:

  > "the Act of 1976 is hereby amended by the substitution of the following section for section 29: Subject to section 75 (1) of this Act, the Minister may, on application to the Minister in that behalf, if he or she thinks fit, *and on payment of the prescribed fee (if any)*, grant to a person, who when making the application makes a declaration in a form approved of for the purposes of this section by the Minister, a licence (operating in the manner specified in subsection (4) of this section) to hunt and kill with firearms, subject to the restrictions contained in section 33 of this Act, and such conditions (if any) as the Minister may attach to the licence, exempted wild mammals (other than hares)".

This provision appears to allow for the imposition of a charge.

Applicants must be qualified persons, as defined above. In practical terms, an applicant for a deer hunting licence is required to provide evidence that he or she has permission and/or a legal entitlement to hunt deer on land on which deer exist in numbers sufficient to justify culling by shooting. The licensing authority requires current written evidence of such permission or legal entitlement, for example, in the form of the permit issued by Coillte Teoranta to nominated stalkers under the terms of Coillte's forest area licensing system, or a current original letter of permission from a landowner. The latter will normally be subject to verification by the local Conservation Ranger.

- **STAG HUNTING (WITH HOUNDS):** irrespective of an open season for deer shooting, it is lawful under licence from the Minister, to hunt deer with stag hounds during any period or periods specified by the licence; section 26 (1) (ii). Special conditions can be attached to such licences, the contravention of which constitutes an offence; section 69 (6).

- **DEFENCE PLEA FOR AGRICULTURE OR FORESTRY:** in any proceedings for an offence under section 23 relating to certain species of protected wild animal, it shall be a defence for the defendant to prove that any capture or killing complained of was urgently necessary in order to stop damage to livestock, poultry, agricultural crop, pen-reared wild birds, other fauna, flora, forestry or a fishery, and that it was not practical for him or her to

The Ward Union and the Co. Down Staghounds both hunt carted deer under licence

seek the prior permission of the Minister for the action; section 23 (8). However it is important to note that this is not a defence where red deer, including hybrids or subspecies, are concerned. If Red deer, or a hybrid or subspecies of red deer, is allegedly causing damage, then the prior permission of the Minister must first be obtained. sections 22 (6), 42 (1), 42 (2), 42 (3), 42 (4) and 42 (6) also apply. Under section 42 (1) and 42 (2), the Minister can authorise an agent to do whatever may be necessary to stop the damage (including capturing or killing), while under section 42 (3), 42 (4) and 42 (6), the owner or occupier of property being damaged may seek permission to deal with the problem himself. In practical terms, this means either the owner/occupier or his agent may apply for what is known as a "Section 42" licence, through the local Conservation Ranger and the National Parks & Wildlife Service. Note: fallow deer, or pure sika deer, are not excluded from a defence under section 23 (8), and may be shot without licence under certain, very specific, circumstances. Red deer or red deer hybrids may not be shot except with prior licence or permission.

- *   **TRESPASS:** in relation to wild deer, it is an offence for a person without the permission of the owner or occupier of the land involved, to hunt on the land using a firearm or other weapon, or a trap, snare, net, birdlime, poison, stupefying bait or other devices or instruments including decoys, lures, lamps and other dazzling devices; or to move or drive wild deer off the land for such purpose; or to carry on the land any firearm or other weapon, instrument or device capable of being used for hunting it; or to shoot over or into the land; section 44 (1) (a), (b), (c) & (d).

- **RIGHT OF CHALLENGE:** the owner, occupier, owner of the sporting rights (or their agents) or the holder of a hunting licence may demand the name and address of a trespasser carrying a weapon or other hunting device, and to refuse or fail to comply with the demand is an offence; section 44 (2) (3). If a defendant claims that he had authority to be on land at the time he was challenged, it is for him to prove it; section 44 (7).

(See below, "Dealing with a suspected poaching incident")

- **TRAPS, SNARES ETC:** it is an offence to hunt deer by means of traps, snares, nets, lines, hooks, arrows, darts, spears or similar devices, or to use birdlime or any similar substance, or any poisonous, poisoned or stupefying bait; section 34 (1) (a), or to set any trap, snare or net for killing or taking any wild bird or any wild mammal on a tree, pole, cairn or other structure in or near a place frequented by wild deer; section 34 (1) (b), or to lay poison or stupefying bait in any such place; section 34 (1) (c). However valid defences may be possible under section 34 (2) (4), which covers trapping or snaring of unprotected wild birds or animals e.g. grey crows, rabbits, rats, mice etc.; or under other Acts, e.g. Protection of Animals (Amendment) Act, 1965 (No. 10 of 1965, sections 7 or 14, or the Protection of Animals Act 1911 (First & Second of George 5, c.27, section 8). Section 34 (1) (a) outlaws bowhunting for wild deer.

Cruel consequences of illegal snaring of deer

- **HUNTING BY NIGHT:** it is an offence to hunt deer between one hour after sunset and one hour before sunrise; section 37 (1), except under special Ministerial licence; or to use a lamp or other dazzling device, except when tagging or marking them or hunting them for educational or scientific purposes under licence from the Minister; section 38. Ministerial licences issued pursuant to section 23 or section 42 of the Act may permit use of a lamp, if specified. Note: it is an offence to mark or tag a wild deer, or to capture it for the purpose of marking or tagging it, except under licence from the Minister; section 32 (1).

- **FIREARMS:** the Minister may make regulations specifying the type and calibre of firearms and ammunition (and prohibiting the use of any other type or calibre) which may be used to hunt wild deer; section 33 (4). The regulation made on July 21st 1977 (S.I. No. 239 of 1977) still prevails, stipulating use of a minimum bullet weight of 55 grains with muzzle energy of 1,637 foot pounds (i.e. .22/250 calibre), although in practical terms this has been overtaken by availability under relaxed conditions of licensing of full bore rifles introduced in 1993. Rifle calibres up to and including .270 inches are now routinely licensed and calibres in excess of .270 have been licensed in individual cases. The minimum permitted calibre in Northern Ireland is .240 or 6 m.m. It is an offence to kill or injure a wild deer with a shotgun, regardless of type of cartridge used; section 33 (4).

Note: the possession, use and carriage of firearms is controlled under the Firearms Acts, 1925 to 2000, and all intending deer stalkers are advised to fully familiarise themselves with those provisions of the Acts which cover firearms used in stalking; see below.

The "European Firearms Pass" was introduced in 1993 under the European Communities (Acquisition and Possession of Weapons and Ammunition) Regulations, 1993 (Statutory Instrument No. 362 of 1993), which provides for a form of licence covering the acquisition, possession, use and carriage of firearms within the European Union (now 25 States) by EU citizens, and inter alia facilitating the transportation of firearms from one Member State to another, where the firearm is licensed to the citizen in his or her own State within the EU.

- **DECOYS AND LURES:** it is an offence to use an electrical or other instrument or appliance (including recording apparatus) emitting or imitating a call, to hunt wild deer except under licence; section 35 (1) (d). It may also be an offence under this section to use any non-mechanical orally or manually operated whistle or other instrument or appliance e.g. deer call, for purposes of hunting deer.

- **USE OF VEHICLES:** it is an offence to hunt deer, or to disturb them for the purpose of hunting them, using a mechanically propelled vehicle, vessel or aircraft, whether it is moving or stationary; section 36 (1), as amended by section 45 of the Wildlife (Amendment) Act, 2000. Thus it is illegal to shoot deer from a vehicle, or to use a vehicle as an aid to shooting. Exceptions are possible under licence; section 36 (2).

- **DRIVING WITH DOGS:** is not a breach of the Wildlife Act, provided that all other legal requirements in relation to hunting of deer are met.

- **WILDLIFE DEALING:** it is an offence to buy, sell or deal in wild deer, either alive or dead, or to engage in taxidermy, without a Wildlife Dealer's Licence; or to be in possession of a wild deer, alive or dead, other than with a Wildlife Dealer's Licence, unless the deer has been lawfully acquired under the various provisions of the Act; section 45 (1), 45 (3), 45 (8), 45 (9 and 47 (1). It is an offence to sell venison to the owner or manager of any hotel, guesthouse, restaurant or club, or for any such person to buy venison, unless one party or the other to the transaction is a licensed wildlife dealer; section 45 (4). The Minister is the party empowered to issue wildlife dealer licences; section 54 of the Wildlife (Amendment) Act, 2000, amending section 48 of the Principal Act.

- **PROSECUTIONS**: only the Minister and the Garda Siochana may prosecute summary proceedings in the District Court for any offence under the Act. Anybody else wishing to do so must have the consent of the Minister or his nominated officer; section 70. Summary proceedings for a trespass offence under section 44 of the Act may be prosecuted by any person who, at the time of the alleged trespass, is either the owner or occupier of the land, or the person entitled to the sporting rights (excluding fishing rights), or the secretary of a "recognised body" (recognised as such under section 44 (5) of the Act) e.g. gun club or game association entitled to the sporting rights; section 44 (4). In the case of the secretary of a recognised body wishing to be in a position to bring a prosecution under Section 44, a notice specifying the lands and stating that the sporting rights over them are reserved to the recognised body must have been published in a national or local newspaper beforehand; section 44 (4) (6). Other than for a breach of section 44, all other prosecutions must be taken by the Minister or the Garda Siochana, except where the consent of the Minister or his nominated officer is obtained.

- **TRANSPORT:** it is an offence to send or carry (by hand or otherwise) any package or parcel containing the body or part of any deer, unless it is conspicuously labelled to indicate the contents; section 51); but it shall be a defence in proceedings under section 51 for a defendant to prove that the package involved contained deer or venison lawfully taken in an open season; section 51 (3).

- **ATTEMPTED OFFENCES AND AIDING AND ABETTING:** it is an offence under the Act to attempt to commit an offence or to aid, abet, counsel, procure, solicit or incite the commission of an offence; section 69 (1); to contravene or fail to comply with regulations made under the Act; section 69 (2); to refuse to give a correct name and address when properly challenged; section 69 (3) (a); to fail to cooperate with an authorised person or a Garda; section 69 (3) (b); to give false information; section 69 (4); to conceal specimens or parts etc. of a deer from an authorised person or a Garda; section 69 (5); to contravene a condition attached to a licence; section 69 (6); or to provide false information or statements in seeking a licence or a permission; section 69 (7).

- **ONUS OF PROOF:** in any proceedings for an offence under the Act it is up to the defendant to prove there was no offence because of the existence of an open season order, a licence or permission, or because the act complained of was either otherwise lawful, or the consequence of an otherwise lawful act; section 71.

- **PENALTIES:** fines not exceeding €634.87 (IR£500) for a first offence, not exceeding €1,269.74 (IR£1,000) for a second offence and not exceeding €1,904.61 (IR£1,500) for a third or subsequent offence are payable on summary conviction for any offence under the Act; section 74 (1), as amended by section 69 of the Wildlife (Amendment) Act, 2000.

Heavier fines (not exceeding €1,904.61 (IR£1,500) on summary conviction or not exceeding €63,486.90 (IR£50,000) on conviction on indictment) apply in certain cases e.g. any offence committed in or in relation to specially protected habitats, e.g. nature reserves (State owned or private, set up under sections 15 or 16), refuges (section 17) or special management agreement areas (section 18); or the illegal hunting or killing or any wild animal declared by Ministerial regulation to be in danger of extinction; section 74 (2) (i) & (iii). Conviction for the illegal hunting or killing of red deer in Kerry for example, may be subject to heavier fines.

Section 69 of the Wildlife (Amendment) Act, 2000 further amends section 74 of the Principal Act by providing for prison sentences ranging from three months to two years in differing circumstances.

On conviction of a person charged with any offence under the Act, the court may, in addition to any monetary penalty or prison sentence, order revocation of deer hunting licence (and disqualify the convicted person from holding a hunting licence for as long as the court sees fit), and may order the surrender and forfeiture of any firearm and ammunition used in the commission of the offence. Such firearms and ammunition may, under the Firearms Acts 1925 to 1971, be destroyed by the Garda Superintendent to whom they must be surrendered; section 75 (1) & (2).

The court may also revoke any Firearm Certificate, and permanently or temporarily disqualify a person convicted of an offence under the Act from holding a Firearms Certificate. The court could conceivably order the forfeiture of a vehicle used in the commission of any offence under section 76 (1) of the Act, which provides for the forfeiture of any firearm, trap, snare, net or "other thing" used in the commission of the offence. Any order for forfeiture is open to appeal before the order can be made. The revocation of a hunting licence or a firearm certificate, temporary or permanent, is not open to appeal under the Wildlife Act 1976 although clearly, the conviction leading to revocation may be.

DEALING WITH A SUSPECTED POACHING INCIDENT

Section 44 of the Wildlife Act, 1976 (as amended) provides that:
Any person who not being the owner or occupier of land:

(a) with a firearm or with a device, instrument or missile mentioned in section 72 (7) of this Act hunts a wild bird or wild animal on the land or moves or drives such a bird or such an animal off the land in order so to hunt it,

(b) enters on the land for the purpose of so hunting wild birds or wild animals,

(c) carries on the land any firearm, net, or other weapon, instrument or device capable of being used for hunting a wild bird or a wild animal, or

(d) shoots over or into the land, without the permission either of the person who is the owner or the occupier of the land or, in case some other person is entitled to enjoy sporting rights over the land, that other person, shall be guilty of an offence. Section 44 also provides that: where a person who is neither the owner nor the occupier of land carries on the land a firearm, other weapon or device (or a part thereof) described in paragraph (c) of subsection (1) of this section, any of the following persons may demand of him (and take when given) his name and address, namely:

(a) the owner or occupier of the land or a person authorised by him to exercise on his behalf the powers exercisable by such owner or occupier under this section,

(b) a person who is entitled to enjoy sporting rights over the land or some other person so authorised by him to exercise on his behalf the powers exercisable by him under this section,

(c) the holder, or a person deemed pursuant to section 29 (5) of this Act to be the holder, of a licence granted under that section; provided that the power conferred by this section on a person mentioned in paragraph (c) of this subsection shall only be exercisable on the production by him of either a current licence granted to him pursuant to the said section 29 or a current firearm certificate granted to him and endorsed in accordance with the requirements of subsection (8) of that section.

This means that any holder of a current licence to hunt deer, or of a current firearms certificate, whether he is the owner, occupier or person entitled to sporting rights over the land in question or not, is entitled to demand of a suspected poacher, his or her name and address. The Act further provides that a person who refuses or who fails to give his correct name and address on such demand being duly made, or who on such demand gives a name and address which is false or misleading, shall be guilty of an offence.

In practical terms, it may not always be expedient or possible to directly challenge a suspected poacher. In these circumstances, it is best to observe the suspected poachers long enough to be able to establish that an offence has been committed.

Write down all details as soon as possible. Precise details of time and date are important – note especially the correct time and date if occurring after midnight. Correct details of the location where the incident occurs, together with details of any vehicles or firearms involved, should be carefully noted. If possible, take photographs.

Notify the nearest Garda Siochana, local Conservation Ranger, the landowner and/or person entitled to the sporting rights (if not you and if known to you), as soon as possible. Keep relevant telephone numbers to hand for this purpose.

Remember when giving details that only what you yourself heard or saw is relevant as evidence. Presumption of an offence is not evidence. Try to find any evidence to back up a case, for instance, a carcase or eviscerated organs.

Thereafter, where it is believed a case is sustainable, a summary prosecution may be brought by the Garda Siochana (on the instructions of the Director of Public Prosecutions), a Conservation Ranger (on behalf of the Minister and the National Parks & Wildlife Service), the owner or occupier of the land concerned or the person entitled to the sporting rights over the land, or in the name of the person who at the relevant time is the secretary of a recognised body which at such time is entitled to enjoy sporting rights over the relevant land. Such an offence shall only be prosecuted by the secretary of a recognised body if (i) prior to the relevant time a notice stating that sporting rights specified in the notice over land so specified have been reserved for the body is published in a newspaper circulating in the area in which the relevant land is situate, and (ii) the land so specified comprises or includes the relevant land. Other categories of complainants do not need to have published a notice of reserved rights.

It is also open to any citizen, under common law, to initiate and prosecute a criminal prosecution.

Although the concept of "Citizen's Arrest" (arrest without warrant) is provided for under section 4 of the Criminal Law Act, 1997, this is not an option in relation to offences or attempted offences under the Wildlife Act, 1976 (as amended) as offences under the Act are not arrestable offences. An arrestable offence is defined in section 2 of the Criminal Law Act, 1997 as "an offence for which a person of full capacity and not previously convicted may, under or by virtue of any enactment, be punished by imprisonment for a term of five years or by a more severe penalty and includes an attempt to commit any such offence". Penalties for offences under the Wildlife Act, 1976 (as amended) are fixed at monetary penalties and a maximum period of imprisonment on conviction of two years.

Any attempt to carry out a citizen's arrest may therefore itself constitute a criminal offence under section 15 of the Non-Fatal Offences Against the Person Act, 1997 (the offence of false imprisonment). Ironically, an offence under section 15 of the Non-Fatal Offences Against the Person Act, 1997 is an arrestable offence; section 15 (3) (b) of the Act provides for sanctions including imprisonment for life on conviction on indictment.

False imprisonment is also a ground for an action in tort (a civil action for recovery of damages, in this context taken by the suspected or allegedly guilty party against the would-be arrestor).

Offences under the Wildlife Act, 1976 (as amended)
are not "arrestable" offences as defined under the
Criminal Law Act, 1997

NORTHERN IRELAND

The Wildlife (Northern Ireland) Order 1985 (S.I. No 171[N.1.2]) covers deer of all species including all hybrids, and includes those on enclosed land where deer not in the wild state are usually kept. Part III, Article 19 of the Order sets out provisions specific to deer. The main provisions of the Order include the following:

- The establishment of Close Seasons
- The establishment of nightly Close times
- The prohibition of a wide range of illegal methods of killing or taking deer e.g. snares, decoys, poisons, night sights or similar, gas or vehicles
- The restriction of the removal of live deer, the marking or tagging of live deer, to persons in possession of a special licence.
- The prohibition of all firearms except a rifle of at least .236 calibre
- All venison must be sold to, by or through licensed game dealers
- In the event of more than one deer being involved in any alleged offence under the Order, the Court may, for the purpose of levying penalties, regard each deer as a separate offence if the charge(s) is (are) proven guilty.

EXCEPTIONS

A person can take or kill deer during the Close season (but not during the nightly Close time) on cultivated land, enclosed pasture, enclosed woodland or gardens, provided:
- he was an authorised person; AND
- he had the reasonable belief that deer of the same species were causing or had caused serious damage to crops or growing timber; AND
- that further serious damage was likely; AND
- his action was necessary to prevent further damage.

(An authorised person is defined as the occupier of the land, OR the person having the right to take or kill deer on that land, OR someone acting with the written authority of either).

There is another exception in that, in the exercise of protecting crops or growing timber, a smooth bore gun can be used provided it is at least 12 bore, and the cartridge used contains either a single non-spherical projectile weighing at least 350 grains, or shot each of which measures at least .203 inches in diameter.

It shall be a defence if a person charged with poaching under the Order can convince the Court that he would have had the consent of the owner or the occupier of the land.

Firearms in Northern Ireland are now covered under the provisions of the Firearms (Northern Ireland) Order 2004, made March 10, 2004, cited as 2004 No. 702 (N.I. 3). See appendix for website address (Legislation, Northern Ireland).

FIREARMS LEGISLATION

The principal act is the Firearms Act, 1925 (as amended) ("the Principal Act"). In practice, the legislation is grouped as the Firearms Acts, 1925 to 2000. However it is important to note that a Statutory instrument introduced in February 2008 provides for "Unrestricted" and "Restricted" firearms, with differing licencing procedures. Although the SI is in force at date of publication, it requires to be supported by certain sections, not as yet commenced, of the Criminal Justice Act 2006. "Unrestricted" firearms includes rifles of calibre up to and including .308. "Restricted" firearms, of calibre greater than .308, may be licenced but subject to different procedures.

The Principal Act, as amended, provides for the following, with all of which the deer hunter, as a licensed firearms user, is expected to be familiar:

Definition of "firearm": "a lethal firearm or other lethal weapon of any description from which any shot, bullet, or other missile can be discharged"; section 1 (1). Section 4 (1) of the Firearms and Offensive Weapons Act, 1990 expanded this definition as follows:

"In the Firearms Acts, 1925 to 1990, "firearm" means –

(a) a lethal firearm or other lethal weapon of any description from which any shot, bullet or other missile can be discharged;

(b) an air gun (which expression includes an air rifle and an air pistol) or any other weapon incorporating a barrel from which metal or other slugs can be discharged;

(c) a crossbow;

(d) any type of stun gun or other weapon for causing any shock or other disablement to a person by means of electricity or any other kind of energy emission;

(e) a prohibited weapon as defined in section 1 (1) of the Firearms Act, 1925;

(f) any article which would be a firearm under any of the foregoing paragraphs but for the fact that, owing to the lack of a necessary component part or parts, or to any other defect or condition, it is incapable of discharging a shot, bullet or other missile or of causing a shock or other disablement (as the case may be);

(g) save where the context otherwise requires, any component part of any article referred to in any of the foregoing paragraphs and, for the purposes of this definition, the following articles shall be deemed to be such component parts as aforesaid.

    (I) telescope sights with a light beam, or telescope sights with an electronic light amplification device or an infra-red device, designed to be fitted to a firearm specified in paragraph (a), (b), (c) or (e), and

    (II) a silencer designed to be fitted to a firearm specified in paragraph (a), (b) or (e)".

Note: whether a "sound moderator" constitutes a "silencer" within the meaning of the Act is an as-yet-undetermined legal point.

Requirement for a firearms certificate: is provided for in section 2 (1); "(*Subject to the exceptions from this section hereinafter mentioned), it shall not be lawful for any person after the commencement of this Act to have in his possession, use, or carry any firearm or ammunition save in so far as such possession, use, or carriage is authorised by a firearms certificate granted under this Act and for the time being in force*".

Who grants the firearms certificate? The firearms certificate is granted by the superintendent of the Garda Siochana of the district in which the applicant habitually resides; section 3 (1). The legislation provides the Garda superintendent *"may"* (not *"shall"*) grant the certificate, he is under no statutory duty to do so. In practice, any decision not to grant a certificate other than in valid circumstances may be amenable to judicial review and unless the superintendent can show just cause why he is declining to grant a certificate, a court order for the granting of a certificate may follow. The Minister for Justice has a limited discretion to grant a firearms certificate to applicants habitually or normally resident outside the State. Certificates may be renewed by a member of the Garda Siochana not below the rank of Sergeant in the district in which the holder of the certificate resides if and so long as he is so authorised in writing by the Superintendent of that district; section 9 of Firearms Act, 1964.

What conditions must the applicant satisfy? The Act provides in section 4 that before granting a firearm certificate to any person under this Act the superintendent of the Gárda Síochána or the Minister (as the case may require) shall be satisfied that such person –
- (a) has a good reason for requiring the firearm in respect of which the certificate is applied for, and
- (b) can be permitted to have in his possession, use, and carry a firearm or ammunition without danger to the public safety or to the peace, and
- (c) is not a person declared by this Act to be disentitled to hold a firearm certificate.

In addition, the applicant must have attained the age of sixteen years at date of application.

The Irish courts have decided that arbitrary conditions, such as a prior requirement for a gun safe, cannot be imposed unilaterally by any superintendent of the Garda Siochana. This is not to suggest that any such proposed conditions, especially those relating to firearms safety inside and outside the home, should be automatically rejected by any applicant for a firearms certificate. As previously indicated, new firearms legislation under consideration at the time of development of this manual is likely to make possession and use of a gun safe mandatory.

Who are "disentitled persons? Section 8 of the Act (as amended by section 17 of the Firearms Act, 1964) provides that the following persons are declared to be disentitled to hold a firearm certificate:
- (a) any person under the age of sixteen years, and
- (b) any person of intemperate habits, and
- (c) any person of unsound mind, and
- (d) any person who has been sentenced by any court in the State to penal servitude or to imprisonment for any term which has not expired or has expired within five years previously for a crime in the course of which a firearm was used or a firearm or an imitation firearm was produced for the apparent purpose of intimidating any person or a threat to use a firearm against any person or property was made, and
- (e) any person who has been sentenced by any court in the State to penal servitude or to imprisonment for any term of not less than three months which has not expired or has expired within five years previously for a crime consisting of or including an assault on any person, and
- (f) any person who is subject to the supervision of the police, and
- (g) any person who is bound by a recognizance to keep the peace or be of good behaviour, a condition of which is that such person shall not have in his possession, or use, or carry any firearm or ammunition.

In what circumstances can a firearms certificate be revoked? A firearms certificate can be revoked by court order (e.g. under section 75 of the Wildlife Act, 1976) following conviction for a stated offence under the law or under section 5 of the Act, by the superintendent of the Garda Siochana of the district in which the holder of a firearm certificate resides is satisfied that the holder of such certificate –

(a)   has no good reason for requiring the firearm to which the certificate relates, or

(b)   is a person who cannot, without danger to the public safety or to the peace, be permitted to have a firearm in his possession, or

(c)   is a person who is declared by this Act to be disentitled to hold a firearm certificate, or

(d)   where the firearm certificate limits the purposes for which the firearm to which it relates may be used, is using such firearm for purposes not authorised by the certificate.

Section 75 of the Wildlife Act, 1976 provides that where a person who holds –

(a)   a firearm certificate which by virtue of section 29 (5) of this Act is deemed to be a licence granted under that section, or

(b)   a firearm certificate granted on the production of a current licence granted by the Minister to the person under section 29 of this Act,

is convicted of an offence under Part II of this Act, the court by which the person in convicted may revoke the certificate mentioned in paragraph (a) of this subsection or the licence mentioned in paragraph (b) of this subsection, as may be appropriate, and disqualify the person from holding such a certificate or licence and such revocation and disqualification shall be for such period as the court thinks appropriate and shall be in addition to any other punishment imposed by the court in respect of the offence.

What is the duration of a firearms certificate? Section 3 (3) of the Act provides that "every firearm certificate shall continue in force until the 31st day of July next after the grant thereof, but a firearm certificate granted may be expressed to commence on the next following 1st day of August and shall in that case be in force on and from such 1st day of August until the next following 31st day of July". In other words, a firearms certificate runs from 1 August to 31 July of the following year.

Are knives covered by legislation? Yes – section 9, subsection (1) of the Firearms and Offensive Weapons Act, 1990 provides that where a person has with him in any public place any knife or any other article which has a blade or which is sharply pointed, he shall be guilty of an offence.

It shall be a defence for a person charged with an offence under subsection (1) to prove that he had good reason or lawful authority for having the article with him in a public place; section 9 (2)
Without prejudice to the generality of subsection (2), it shall be a defence for a person charged with an offence under subsection (1) to prove that he had the article with him for use at work or for a recreational purpose; section 9 (3)

DOGS

All deer hunters should have access to a trained tracking dog for purposes of following up and finding shot deer. Access to a tracking dog is a condition of Coillte Teoranta's forest area licence.

Ownership and keeping of dogs, whether as pets or as working dogs, is regulated by the Control of Dogs Act, 1986, and dog-owning deer hunters should be familiar with the provisions of the Act.

It is an offence to keep a dog without the requisite dog licence; Section 2 of the Act.

The occupier of any premises where a dog is found is deemed to be the person who keeps the dog unless he proves that:

    (a)   he is not the owner of the dog, and
    (b)   the dog was kept on the premises either—
            (i)   without his knowledge, or
            (ii)   by some other person who had a licence for the dog.

Dog licenses may not be issued to persons aged under 16 years; section 4.

Dogs must be kept under "effectual control" at all times and in all places; section 9. This does not necessarily mean on a leash.

If a dog worries livestock, the owner or any other person in charge of the dog shall be guilty of an offence unless it is established that at the material time the dog worried the livestock for the purpose of removing trespassing livestock and that having regard to all the circumstances the action was reasonable and necessary; section 9 (2).
Section 16 of the Act provides that:

(1) A dog warden may –

    (a)   where he has reasonable grounds for believing that a person is committing, or has committed, an offence under this Act or under any regulation or bye-law made thereunder, request of the person his name and address and may request that any information given be verified;
    (b)   seize any dog and detain it in order to ascertain whether an offence under this Act is being or has been committed and may enter any premises (other than a dwelling) for the purposes of such seizure and detention;
    (c)   enter any premises (other than a dwelling) for the purpose of preventing or ending –
            (i)   an attack by a dog on any person, or
            (ii)   the worrying of livestock;
    (d)   enter any premises (other than a dwelling)-
            (i)   which are registered in accordance with regulations made under section 19 of this Act, or

        (ii) where he has reasonable grounds for believing that more than five dogs which are aged over four months are kept, and therein examine such dogs as he may find there and the kennels or part of the premises in which the dogs are kept;

(e)   request any person who owns, is in charge of, or is in possession of a dog to produce, as the case may be, a dog licence or a general dog licence, within ten days of the date of the request, for examination by the dog warden.

(2) A dog warden, in exercising a power of entry into any premises under this Act, may bring with him into such premises such other persons as he believes to be necessary for the purpose of assisting him in the exercise of his powers and functions under this Act and the dog warden and any such other person may take with them into the premises such equipment as they consider to be necessary.

(3) Any person who –

(a) obstructs or impedes a dog warden in the exercise of his functions under this Act, or

(b)   refuses to give his name and address to a dog warden when requested so to do, or who gives a name or address which is false or misleading when so requested, shall be guilty of an offence and shall be liable on summary conviction to –

       (i) in case the offence is an offence under paragraph (a) of this subsection, a fine not exceeding €835 (£500), or to imprisonment for a term not exceeding one month, or, at the discretion of the court, to both such fine and such imprisonment, or

       (ii) in case the offence is an offence under paragraph (b) of this subsection, a fine not exceeding €127 (£100).

(4) Where a member of the Garda Síochána is of opinion that a person is committing or has committed an offence under this section, he may arrest the person without warrant. Section 21 of the Act attaches strict liability to the owner of any dog which causes damage or injury to livestock or to humans, viz.

S. 21   (1): The owner of a dog shall be liable in damages for damage caused in an attack on any person by the dog and for injury done by it to any livestock; and it shall not be necessary for the person seeking such damages to show a previous mischievous propensity in the dog, or the owner's knowledge of such previous propensity, or to show that such injury or damage was attributable to neglect on the part of the owner.

      (2)   Where livestock are injured by a dog on land on to which they had strayed, and either the dog belonged to the occupier of the land or its presence on the land was authorised by the occupier, a person shall not be liable under this section in respect of injury done to the livestock, unless the person caused the dog to attack the livestock.

      (3)   A person is liable in damages for any damage caused by a dog kept on any premises or structure to a person trespassing thereon only in accordance with the rules of law relating to liability for negligence.

Finally, be aware that a Conservation Ranger or member of the Garda Siochana has the power to seize any dog used to hunt deer illegally, or used in the commission of any offence under the Wildlife Act, 1976 (as amended), under section 72 of the Principal Act, as amended by section 65 of the Wildlife (Amendment) Act, 2000.

Is your dog safe with sheep?

TRESPASS AND THE OCCUPIERS' LIABILITY ACT, 1995

Persons trespassing on another's property for whatever purpose are subject to the common law rules regarding trespass, nuisance and damage to property. Note also the provisions of section 44 (1) of the Wildlife Act, 1976 (above) as amended by section 50 of the Wildlife (Amendment) Act, 2000.

However most legitimate deer hunters are likely to be defined as "visitors" to land within the meaning of the Occupiers' Liability Act, 1995, i.e.

    (a)   an entrant, other than a recreational user, who is present on premises at the invitation, or with the permission, of the occupier or any other entrant specified in paragraph (a), (b) or (c) of the definition of "recreational user",

    (b)   an entrant, other than a recreational user, who is present on premises by virtue of an express or implied term in a contract, and

    (c)   an entrant as of right,

        while he or she is so present, as the case may be, for the purpose for which he or she is invited or permitted to be there, for the purpose of the performance of the contract or for the purpose of the exercise of the right, and includes any such entrant whose presence on premises has become unlawful after entry thereon and who is taking reasonable steps to leave.

"Recreational user" means an entrant who, with or without the occupier's permission or at the occupier's implied invitation, is present on premises without a charge (other than a reasonable charge in respect of the cost of providing vehicle parking facilities) being imposed for the purpose of engaging in a recreational activity.

"Trespasser" means an entrant other than a recreational user or visitor.

Varying levels of duty of care apply as between visitors, recreational users and trespassers.

The Act imposes a common law duty of care towards visitors as follows (section 3):

    (1)   An occupier of premises owes a duty of care ("the common duty of care") towards a visitor thereto except in so far as the occupier extends, restricts, modifies or excludes that duty in accordance with section 5.

    (2)   In this section "the common duty of care" means a duty to take such care as is reasonable in all the circumstances (having regard to the care which a visitor may reasonably be expected to take for his or her own safety and, if the visitor is on the premises in the company of another person, the extent of the supervision and control the latter person may reasonably be expected to exercise over the visitor's activities) to ensure that a visitor to the premises does not suffer injury or damage by reason of any danger existing thereon.

An occupier's liability may be extended, modified, restricted or excluded under section 5 of the Act, which provides as follows:

(1) An occupier may by express agreement or notice extend his or her duty towards entrants under sections 3 and 4.

(2) (a) Subject to this section and to section 8, an occupier may by express agreement or notice restrict, modify or exclude his or her duty towards visitors under section 3.

(b) Such a restriction, modification or exclusion shall not bind a visitor unless—

(i) it is reasonable in all the circumstances, and

(ii) in case the occupier purports by notice to so restrict, modify or exclude that duty, the occupier has taken reasonable steps to bring the notice to the attention of the visitor.

(c) For the purposes of paragraph (b) (ii) an occupier shall be presumed, unless the contrary is shown, to have taken reasonable steps to bring a notice to the attention of a visitor if it is prominently displayed at the normal means of access to the premises.

(3) In respect of a danger existing on premises, a restriction, modification or exclusion referred to in subsection (2) shall not be taken as allowing an occupier to injure a visitor or damage the property of a visitor intentionally or to act with reckless disregard for a visitor or the property of a visitor.

(4) In determining for the purposes of subsection (3) whether or not an occupier has acted with reckless disregard, regard shall be had to all the circumstances of the case including, where appropriate, the matters specified in subsection (2) of section 4.

(5) Where injury or damage is caused to a visitor or property of a visitor by a danger of which the visitor had been warned by the occupier or another person, the warning is not, without more, to be treated as absolving the occupier from liability unless, in all the circumstances, it was enough to enable the visitor, by having regard to the warning, to avoid the injury or damage so caused.

It should be noted that the standard Coillte Teoranta forest area licence and related permit limit Coillte's liability (see appendix for conditions of standard licence). Similarly, private owners and occupiers of land who grant permission to hunt wild deer on their property may limit liability to visitors under the foregoing section 5.

CHAPTER X

CARCASE HANDLING AND FOOD SAFETY

Once a deer has been shot it then becomes a food product and the way in which it is handled is not only of critical importance to the final consumer but is also subject to legislative control. The meat is known as venison and is particularly low in fat with a dressed carcase percentage of about 5% compared to 20% for cattle and sheep. Also 50% of deer fat is the much healthier polyunsaturated form compared with about 5% in domestic stock.

The deer carcase should first be bled; this is done by sticking a knife into the front of the chest above the end of the breastbone and between the first two ribs. This severs the anterior vena cava, the major vein in the chest and allows the carcase to bleed out. Ideally the carcase should be lifted by the hind legs but this is not always possible and in such cases the head and heck should be placed at an angle below the line of the body to aid drainage. Very often if the animal has been shot in the chest or liver there will be considerable bleeding into the body cavities with a resultant decrease in the amount seen to leave the body following bleeding. This is acceptable as the purpose of bleeding a carcase is to reduce the amount of blood in the muscles. A poorly bled deer will decompose rapidly and will be condemned at the game-processing establishment upon inspection.

Traditionally the gut contents of a deer carcase are removed at the place where the animal is shot, together with the red offal and head if the animal is not going to be sold into the food chain. This is still applies when no abnormal features are found by the trained hunter on examining the body and viscera. However these are required if abnormal characteristics are found in which case the carcase has to undergo full veterinary inspection. The red offal consists of heart, lungs, liver and kidneys.

Removal of the gut contents greatly reduces the weight when bringing a dead deer back to the vehicle, however consideration should be given to delaying this process until the animal is in the larder or at least until the carcase is near the vehicle, as this minimizes contamination from soil, ground water and plant materials.

Removal of the lower legs should also be delayed until presentation at the place of final skinning. The green offal, gut, spleen, bladder and gravid uterus in the case of heavily pregnant females should be examined for abnormalities and buried on the stalking ground.

There is EU Legislation (Regulation No EC 1774/2002) which deals with the disposal of animal by-products not intended for human consumption. While this legislation prohibits burial of carcase parts the Regulation does not apply to parts of wild animals provided they are not suspected of being infected with diseases communicable to humans or animals, or are parts being used for game trophies. Therefore provided the hunter is satisfied that the animal does not have a disease which is transmissible to man or animals he can bury the offal. Such offal should be buried deep enough to prevent it being dug up by carnivorous animals and in an area which will not lead to contamination of the water table or create any other environmental nuisance. If it is suspected that the animal is suffering from a disease which is communicable to man or animals, then any animal by-products must be disposed of as a Category 1 material which in this country means they must be sent of a Category 1 rendering plant for processing. In practical terms this might mean disposing of the offal through a game dealer.

To eviscerate the carcase the animal is laid on its back, preferably with its head uphill. The neck is then incised and the oesophagus freed from its position alongside the trachea or windpipe. It is then either knotted or sealed with an elastic band. The abdominal cavity is then incised from the back of the breastbone back towards the pelvis. Care must be taken not to puncture the guts within the abdominal cavity. This is particularly important if the process does not take place immediately after death, as the continuation of fermentation of the gut contents will cause the rumen to swell considerably. The previously knotted oesophagus should then be pulled through the chest and the guts gently removed form the abdomen. The rectum should be excised from outside the body in the case of the male deer, cutting also around the vulva in the case of the female. These should then be pulled through into the abdominal cavity and then removed.

The whole process is easier, cleaner and more hygienic if it can be completed while the animal is hanging by its hind legs in a larder, but it can be done by hanging the animal from a tree. However this must be done quickly as the heat generated by the fermenting gut contents will render the meat unsuitable for human consumption.

If the animal is not intended for processing through a game dealer then the red offal should be removed at this stage, and the carcase can then be skinned. Hunters will find it much easier to skin a deer while the body is still warm. If the meat is for home consumption or for occasional free distribution among friends the carcase is unlikely to be professionally inspected for disease or other abnormalities. In this case the hunter should have a good understanding of disease recognition. This is important not only for the consumer of the venison, but also information gathered will facilitate better wild deer management and possibly will also be of interest and

Even under field conditions carcases can be handled in a hygienic manner

value to neighbouring landowners. Some of these specific disease conditions are considered in detail later in the chapter. The carcase should also be examined for its general body condition and any evidence of contamination.

The drag. Care must be taken not to contaminate the carcase while moving it to the vehicle

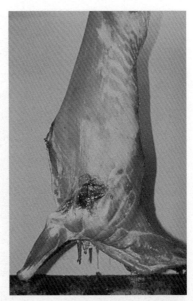

Typical carcase damage from heart/lung shot

CARCASES UNFIT FOR HUMAN CONSUMPTION

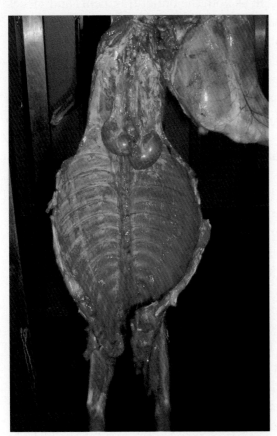

Severe emaciation will lead to condemnation of carcase

At certain times of the year particularly following the rut in male deer and later in the winter in pregnant females, carcases can be in poor condition, with very little discernable body fat and the venison is often dark in colour. This is not the same as in an emaciated carcase where there is considerable wasting of the muscles. In these cases the carcase does not set where hung and the surface of the meat remains damp to the touch, even sticky. These carcases should be condemned as unfit for human consumption.

The greatest cause for condemnation of all or part of a wild deer carcase is damage and contamination due to the gunshot injury. The way to minimize this damage is to shoot the animal in the head or neck but for the reasons outlined elsewhere in the manual these are not the target areas of choice for any but the most experienced of stalkers.

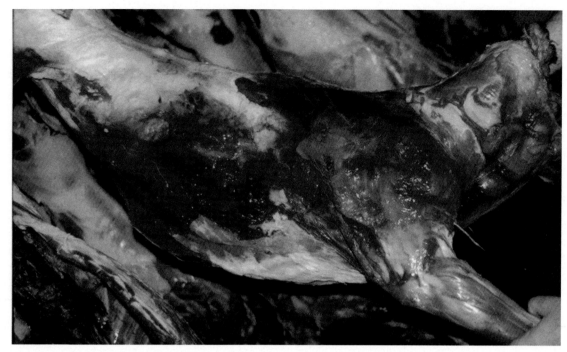

Shoulder-shot deer with severe 'blood splash', requiring extensive trimming

Deer are shot with expanding rifle ammunition. The heavier bullet weights tend to exit the body more easily whereas the light minimum calibres like .22/250 often disintegrate on touching bone and cause considerable damage as both the bullet fragments and pieces of shattered bone fly through the body. The resultant bleeding and bruising makes these affected areas unsaleable. Severe shoulder damage following a chest shot will normally result in a condemnation of the front end. Contamination with intestinal contents can result from gut and liver shots, quartering chest shots and poor evisceration technique. It may also result from bad practice during transportation. Faecal contamination will be dealt with in greater detail later. Occasionally carcases are presented at a game dealer following a road traffic accident. These are easily detected by the pattern of bruising when the animal is skinned and are always condemned.

A stalker may notice an unpleasant odour when skinning a carcase. Very often this is associated with the stag in the rut. The novice hunter should be aware that although this odour may disappear when the carcase is hung for a couple of days it may reappear upon cooking. The fallow buck also has a pungent smelling exudates from its prostrate gland so care should be taken when removing this from the carcase. Smells may also be associated with abscessation which is often as the result of injury. Small abscesses are an indication for condemnation.

Putrefaction of a carcase is a common cause for condemnation both at the game dealer and for the deer hunter processing this meat at home. It causes a foul smell and of course the spoilt meat is not fit for human consumption. This is particularly a problem early in the deer-hunting season when ambient temperatures are high. Where the stalker does not have access to chilling facilities it is compounded by flyblow, where flies lay their eggs on the exposed meal, to develop as maggots. Even if eggs are laid on a carcase while in transport to a larder, they will not develop if the chiller is at the correct temperature. Areas to be cheeked for fly strike are the hole where the anus have been removed and the top section of the abdominal opening on a carcase hung by the back legs.

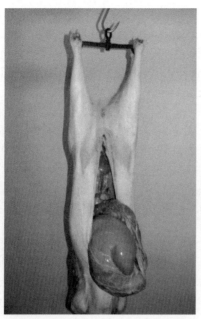

Where possible, evisceration should take place in the larder

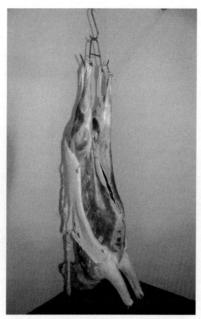

Skinning is always easier if done when the carcase is warm

Faecal contamination from gut contents due to poor evisceration technique, or to contamination from mud from dragging a carcase should all be trimmed away. Gross faecal contamination can also result from bullet damage. In many cases the shock produced from such a wound can draw the ruminal and guy contents into the chest cavity or large muscle masses. In such cases the whole carcase is condemned.

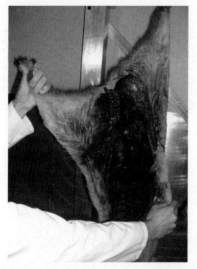

Example of gross faecal contamination due to poor evisceration technique

As mentioned earlier It if is suspected that the animal is suffering from a disease which is communicable to man or animals, then any animal by-products must be disposed of as a Category 1 material which in Ireland means they must be sent of a Category 1 Rendering Plant for processing. In practical terms this might mean disposing of the offal through a game dealer.

Legislation allows for the removal of the head and feet prior to inspection. However stalkers who sell carcases should be aware that generalised tuberculosis, manifesting as lesions in more than one region of the body, is a cause for carcase condemnation and if a suspect lesion is found in the lung and the head is not available for inspection, then the whole carcase is classed as unfit for human consumption.

Normal position of retropharyngeal lymph nodes in a deer's throat

Normal mediastinal lymph node in lungs

Normal mesenteric lymph nodes in gut

Stalkers should aim to deliver carcases to the game processing facility within 12 hours of killing, however if this is not possible it can be taken to a collection centre (larder) for chilling, from which is must be transferred to the processing facility within a further 12 hours.

THE GAME LARDER

The function of the game larder is to allow the carcase to cool under hygiene and fly proof conditions. It is very important that carcases are well ventilated. The chilling room not only refrigerates venison but also dries the carcase with a fan circulating cold air.

The temperature should be between -1 and +7 degrees if stored for up to 7 days and between -1 and +1 degrees if stored for up to 15 days. Carcases will remain damp if there is no air circulation and mould will develop, particularly inside the chest and pelvic cavity where circulation is particularly poor. The hanging of game allows the meat to tenderise and the flavour to develop. The drying of the carcase will cause it to lose weight.

The home larder must have a concrete or tiled floor with a non-slip finish, which is sloped to a floor gully. There should be a trap on the gully to collect hair, fat and blood clots from the carcase. These gullys must be cleaned regularly and certainly after every session in the larder. Walls must be of an impervious washable surface, painted white to reveal any dirt or blood. All work surfaces must be of stainless steel or plastic to allow proper cleaning. A fly electrocuter should be installed. A deer larder should have a hoist for lifting large carcases, particularly if red deer are being handled.

Hand washing facilities and hoses should be available. Water used for washing surfaces must be of a standard suitable for human drinking water. An effective detergent disinfectant must be used to wash all surfaces after the larder has been used. It must be capable of breaking down the fat residues which accumulate on the floor and work surface. Effluent should go to mains sewerage or into a septic tank.

A first aid kit must be available in all game larders.

A small refrigerated larder is a good investment even for the amateur stalker.
Consider pooling resources with a stalking companion or group

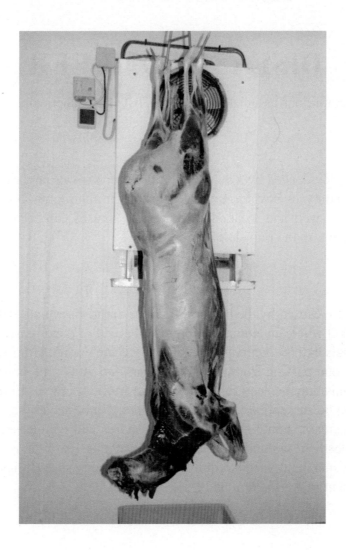

Mould growth will be seen in carcases which have been washed but not dried properly in a chiller

DISEASES OF DEER

Specific disease conditions associated with deer, listed alphabetically:

Actinomycosis

This is a condition evidenced by a swelling on the deer's lower jaw, caused by the entry of a bacteria Actinomyces bovis following abrasions in the mouth. Pus builds up in the bone causing it to swell and weaken. Discharging sinuses can form either inside the mouth or discharging to the outside of the jaw.

Anthrax

Anthrax is a disease caused by the bacteria Bacillus anthracis which exists in spore form generally in the soil where an animal has previously died of the disease. The condition is rare in farm animals in this country. The clinical signs are normally those of sudden death with dark tarry blood passing from the mouth, anus and vulva in females, unfortunately the same symptoms may be seen following a road traffic accident. Both fallow and red deer are known to be susceptible, though it is unlikely to be seen by a hunter. If anthrax is suspected the carcase should not be opened as spores will be released and the disease can also cause death in humans. It is mentioned in this list as it is a scheduled and notifiable disease making it a legal requirement for anybody suspecting anthrax to report it to the Department of Agriculture and Food.

Arthritis

Arthritis is the inflammation of a joint. Chronic arthritis will lead to rejection of a joint and surrounding tissues but acute septic arthritis with pus inside the joint should lead to carcase rejection.

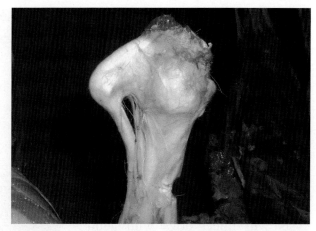

Arthritis, leading to swelling of the hock joint

Chronic Wasting Disease

Chronic Wasting Disease (CWD) is a disease currently recognised only in North America and recently in Korea. It is mentioned here only as a potential pathogen of Irish deer and for the interest of deerstalkers as it is widely written about in deer journals and hunting publications. It is one of a group of transmissible spongiform encephalopathies of which BSE is the best known in Europe. They are a group of central nervous (brain) diseases which have a prion protein as their infectious agent. It is thought to be related to scrapie, a sheep disease found here. Unlike BSE, there is as yet no evidence that CWD can cause disease in humans. CWD has been diagnosed in whitetail and mule deer and Rocky Mountain elk, the latter being closely related to both red and sika deer. Symptoms are of weight loss and altered behaviour, leading to death in all cases. Little is known about the spread of the disease though it is far more infectious than BSE.

Under existing legislation in Ireland, no part of a deer carcase is considered to be specific risk material in relation to BSE. Only cattle, sheep and contain SRM. Although there is no evidence that European deer species are infected with any transmissible spongiform encephalopathy, hunters are advised to avoid contamination of meat with brain or spinal cord tissue. Hunters splitting heads in the preparation of trophies are advised to use a separate saw for this purpose and not the saw used in the normal butchering process.

Chronic Wasting Disease has not been identified in Irish deer species.
above: America White-tail deer with severe CWD.

Cysticercus Tenuicollis

While cleaning out a carcase the deer hunter will sometimes observe a fluid-filled cyst either in the abdominal cavity or attached to one of the internal organs. This is a tapeworm cyst (the intermediate stage of a dog or fox tapeworm). These cysts are thin-walled and filled with fluid. Ingestion of these cysts will infect dogs with adult tapeworms so they should be excised and discarded safely.

Tapeworm cyst attached to mesentry in sika stag's abdomen

External Parasites

(I)   Ticks: commonly seen on deer. Ixodes ricinus has a life cycle which lasts up to three years though only a few days at a time are spent on the animal. It is not host-specific in that any stage can be completed on any host, cattle and sheep being the most common. The adult female feeds on the first host for about two weeks and drops to the ground to lay its eggs. These adults are the ticks most commonly recognized by stalkers - large grey blood-filled insects with eight legs. They can attach anywhere to the body but generally are to be found in the groin and under the front legs. The eggs then hatch out in the grass and feed on hosts such as small rodents and birds for about a week. They fall off, moult and remain on the ground over the winter. The nymph stage then emerges, feeding on a third host before changing to an adult and completing the life cycle.

(II) Keds: the deer ked, Lipoptena cervi, is a relatively large blood-sucking parasite, commonly seen in the coats of red deer in Scotland. Initially winged, they lose their wings when they find a host deer. Deer hunters can often pick them up in their hair when handling carcases. Although not generally known in Ireland, some instances have recently been reported in Donegal.

(III) Warble fly: Hypoderma diana is a different species to that found in cattle and there is no cross infection between the two. Again, this is a common parasite in Scotland, affecting mainly red deer but other species can be affected. This has been reported to occur in red deer in Co. Donegal. The adult female fly lays her eggs on the deer's coat, they penetrate the skin and migrate to the deer's back where they encyst and form large nodules under the skin. From these lumps an adult fly will emerge. They cause damage to the hide of the affected deer though causing little distress to the animal itself. The larvae are seen under in the subcutaneous tissues when the carcase is skinned, particularly during December, January and February.

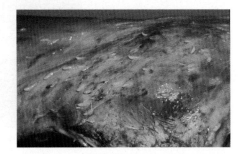

Severe warble infestation in red deer carcase

(IV)   Lice: lice of the species Damalinia and Trichodectes are found in all species of deer. They are a natural parasite and cause little in the way of problems to the host. They are normally just found around the head but when the winter coat grows they spread out across the body. They are found in higher numbers in old or sick animals which tend to moult later and spend less time grooming themselves and thereby removing their louse burden.

(V)   Nasal Bot Fly: common in Britain, there are two species of the Cephenemyia fly that affect deer. The adult fly lays its eggs on the nostrils and the larvae migrate up and develop in the nasal cavities. They can cause considerable distress in affected animals before they leave the nostrils and pupate on the ground.

Foot and Mouth Disease

Foot and Mouth Disease is probably the most contagious of all animal diseases, and had been consigned to history in Ireland until the outbreak of 2001. It is a scheduled and notifiable disease, though from the very mild nature of the symptoms of the disease in deer it is unlikely to be diagnosed by a hunter. The symptoms are far more severe in cattle and pigs and it is in these species that an initial outbreak diagnosis is likely to be made, possibly in a meat factory. As soon as such a case is confirmed all deer stalking in the region is likely to be suspended. Infected animals of all species form vesicles or blisters on the tongue, feet and anal areas, these burst and the virus is then released, spreading in the air and on feet and vehicles. Deer are likely to become infected, but because the lesions are very small and subtle the dose of virus that they excrete is normally insufficient to infect other animals in extensive field conditions.

The decision on whether to cull deer in a FMD infected area is contentious. In 2001 in the Cooley Peninsula, the decision was taken to cull all susceptible species. Several hundred feral goats were killed but only a small number of deer. In the UK the decision was taken not to interfere with the deer as it was decided that attempts to cull around an infected premises was likely to spread the deer onto neighbouring properties. This policy proved itself with the fact that there is no reservoir of infection left in the deer population there. This 'leave alone' policy was adopted in Israel in 1985 when mountain gazelles became infected and the disease was found to gradually die out.

Fractures

These injuries, usually old, are often of interest to the stalker. Often resulting from road traffic accidents, these injuries often heal well and are usually only noticed when the dead animal is being processed. Calves often lose feet if caught by a mower in long grass. Healed injuries following gunshot wounds are also fairly common. There is evidence of contra lateral antler deformity in male deer following limb fractures, i.e. a fracture of a left leg will give rise to abnormal antler growth on the right side in the following year.

Despite losing a limb, deer can often survive on three legs. This injury had healed well

Liver Fluke

The liver fluke has an indirect life cycle requiring it to pass through the water snail, Limnaea truncatula. There is a difference in susceptibility depending on the deer species and the areas being grazed. Sika deer are very resistant and one rarely finds lesions in their livers, while in Scotland liver fluke is considered to be one of the major population control factors in roe deer. In the Irish deer species the signs of fluke damage in the liver is a mottled appearance to the surface and a thickening of the bile ducts when the livers are incised. Live flukes will often be seen within these ducts. The parasite rarely causes significant disease in deer here, though badly affected livers should be condemned.

Lungworm

While a major cause of disease in farmed deer, lungworm also causes disease more sporadically in wild deer, particularly in calves and fawns grazing pasture with cattle.

Basal cell tumour on surface skin of deer

Tuberculosis

There are two types of tuberculosis found in deer, bovine tuberculosis caused by Mycobacterium bovis and avian tuberculosis caused by Mycobacterium avium. It is impossible for the hunter to differentiate between the two. As bovine tuberculosis is a scheduled and notifiable disease all suspected cases should be reported to your local District Veterinary Office, the telephone numbers of which are given below.

DISTRICT VETERINARY OFFICES

Carlow	(059) 9170022	Longford	(043) 50020
Cavan	(049) 4368200	Louth	(041) 9870086
Clare	(065) 6866042	Mayo	(094) 9035300
Cork North/East	(021) 4851400	Meath	(046) 9079030
Cork South/West	(023) 36200	Monaghan	(042) 9748800
Donegal	(074) 9145990	Offaly	(0506) 46037
Dublin/Wicklow East	(01) 4149900	Roscommon	(090) 6630100
Galway	(091) 507600	Sligo	(071) 9155030
Kerry	(066) 7145052	Tipperary North	(067) 50014
Kildare/Wicklow West	(045) 873035	Tipperary South	(062) 80100
Kilkenny	(056) 7772400	Waterford	(051) 301700
Laois	(0502) 74400	Westmeath	(044) 39034
Leitrim	(071) 9620030	Wexford	054) 42008
Limerick	(061) 208500		

Common courtesy dictates that the owner of the land also be informed, particularly if cattle are being farmed.

Avian tuberculosis causes clinical disease in deer but is not a significant pathogen in cattle. Differentiation between this and the bovine form when a suspected case is presented requires culture of the lymph nodes. Care must therefore be taken not to immediately jump to conclusions as to whether deer have bovine tuberculosis (bTB) when a suspected lesion is found. Bovine tuberculosis can cause disease in humans so precautions must be taken when handling a suspected infected carcase.

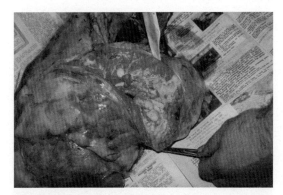

Pus-filled lungs in TB-positive fallow deer

TB abscesses attached to liver, later cultured as bovine tuberculosis. All abscesses must be regarded as potential tuberculosis lesions

The bacteria usually enters the body either by the respiratory or oral route. A general indication of the route of infection can be guessed at by the site of the lesions in affected lymph nodes, those in the lungs and retropharyngeal lymph nodes indicating infection via the respiratory system and infection in the mesenteric lymph nodes around the gut suggesting an alimentary route of infection. This is not however a hard and fast rule as respiratory-infected deer can cough up and swallow infected sputum and therefore develop lesions in the gut. The majority of deer with respiratory system lesions culture positive for bovine type lesions while those with alimentary lesions are usually infected with avian tuberculosis. In some animals infection may be present for long periods without progressing while in others it may be very acute with rapid weight loss and large abscesses developing. All abscesses in deer should alert the stalker to the possibility of infection.

In recent years much research has been done in Ireland and abroad in the role played by wildlife in the spread of bTB to cattle. It is proven that there is a high incidence of bTB in badgers and that control of the badger population in certain areas has reduced the incidence of TB amongst the local cattle population. However the way that the bacteria behave in the badger's body is very different to the disease progression in deer. Badgers excrete the infection in their urine and can contaminate pasture over a wide area.

The incidence of bTB in wild deer is very much lower. Little research has been done in this area though there are a number of projects currently being undertaken. In 1984 Dr K. Dodd of University College Dublin published a paper showing an incidence of 3.8% of bovine tuberculosis in the red offal of 130 deer carcases from Co Wicklow. Recent data from culled deer undergoing veterinary examination prior to processing in a wild game plant in Wicklow shows negligible levels of the disease. This underlines the difficulty in identifying lesions.

When examining a carcase for tuberculosis the following areas should be examined, though as stated earlier, abscessation can occur anywhere:

(a) Retropharyngeal lymph nodes
(b) Mediastinal lymph nodes
(c) Lung tissue
(d) Liver tissue
(e) Mesenteric lymph nodes

Tuberculosis lesion in retropharyngeal lymph node, fallow deer

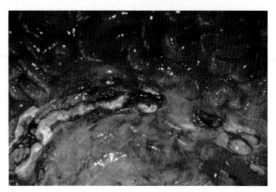

The mesenteric lymph chain from this red deer hind cultured positive for avian tuberculosis

The position of the major lymph nodes is shown in the photographs accompanying this text. They are normally about 1-2 cm in diameter and are dark grey in colour.

Sample Taking

Little is known of the disease status of the Irish wild deer population. They are generally considered to be very healthy. Deer hunters are in the front line when it comes to the recognition of disease processes. Photographs and records should be taken where possible. Samples can also be taken and sent for examination. Although freezing of samples make them useless for histology, tissue samples can be preserved in formalin. Samples of pus can be taken with sterile swabs. Organs or possibly the whole carcase may be submitted to a laboratory. At all stages the landowner should be involved if it is suspected that there is a risk of infectious disease. The farmer may wish to consult with his veterinary surgeon.

When handling the carcase of a deer the hunter must always remember that he is dealing with a food product. Almost uniquely these days it is one of the few red meat sources that can commonly go from forest to fork without any supervision from professional meat inspectors or food hygiene controls. It is important that the hunter understands his obligations in this regard.

Work surfaces must be kept scrupulously clean

As well as the specific diseases mentioned earlier, health wild deer also carry organisms with the potential to cause disease in humans from bacteria naturally found in their gut and on their skin. These bacteria have the potential to cause food poisoning or worse if they are allowed to contaminate and multiply on venison. The most common species of bacteria involved would be Ecolab, Salmonella and Campylobacter. Symptoms of food poisoning include vomiting, diarrhoea, high temperature and stomach cramps. They can last several days and in some cases can give rise to long term health problems and sever disease in those that are young or elderly, or people with suppressed immune systems.

Try to ensure that deer carcases are kept clean. When bringing the shot animal to the vehicle it is preferable to leave the internal organs in the body when moving it to prevent contamination of the abdominal cavity with soil and debris. If larder facilities are available nearby the evisceration should ideally be performed there. The carcase should be kept dry and clean where possible. DO not drag it through streams; lift it over muddy areas and watercourse. If evisceration is to be performed in the field, use latex gloves as handwashing facilities are unlikely to be available. Keep the incision in the abdominal wall as small and as neat as possible, and be prepared to trim away any of the soiled parts of exposed muscle before butchering.

Home Carcase Preparation for Domestic Consumption and occasional free supply to friends

- Carcases must be hung off the ground
- Carcases must not touch one another
- Skinned carcases must be hung separately from unskinned carcases
- All cutting boards, knives and counters must be cleaned and sterilized in between use, particularly if these are later to be used to handle cooked foods
- Hands should be washed regularly, particularly under the nails, before and after skinning, before and after butchering and before and after cleaning the carcase preparation area. Hands should be washed particularly thoroughly after using the toilet.

Remember home-prepared venison cannot be sold. It is the hunter's friends and family that will be consuming the meat so produced.

Never store prepared raw venison or any raw meat for that matter, with cooked meat. In a fridge, store at the bottom so that meat juices cannot drip onto other foods.

Further information on the safe handling of food information is available from the Food Safety Authority of Ireland, Abbey Court, Lower Abbey Street, Dublin 1. Advice Line: 1890 33 66 77, Website: www.fsai.ie

When handling a deer carcase it is important to remember that it is ultimately a food product, for human consumption

EU Food Hygiene Regulations Applicable to Wild Game

Regulation (EC) No 852/2004 and Regulation (EC) No 853/2004 set out detailed rules for the placing of wild game and wild game meat on the market. These do not apply to either hunted game for private domestic consumption by the hunter or to the occasional free supply (by the hunter) of surplus game to friends.

Under the EC Regulations there is provision for the establishment of separate National Rules for the supply of small quantities of wild game and/or wild game meat directly to the final consumer or to local retail establishments directly supplying the final consumer. Hunters wishing to place wild game or wild game meat on the market will have to comply with either National Rules (these will be established in 2007) or the full Regulations depending on the quantity and destination involved.

The Regulations or National Rules are in addition to, and not in substitution of, the Wildlife Act of 1976, as amended.

A key aspect of compliance with the EU Regulations/National Rules is the requirement for hunters to be trained and the following extract from the Regulations details the key competencies:

REGULATION (EC) No 853/2004

SECTION IV: WILD GAME MEAT

CHAPTER I: TRAINING OF HUNTERS IN HEALTH AND HYGIENE

1: Persons who hunt wild game with a view to placing it on the market for human consumption must have sufficient knowledge of the pathology of wild game, and of the production and handling of wild game and wild game meat after hunting, to undertake an initial examination of wild game on the spot.

2: It is however enough if at least one person of a hunting team has the knowledge referred to in point 1. References in this Section to a 'trained person' are references to that person.

3: The trained person could also be the gamekeeper or the game manager if he or she is part of the hunting team or located in the immediate vicinity of where hunting is taking place. In the latter case, the hunter must present the wild game to the gamekeeper or game manager and inform them of any abnormal behaviour observed before killing.

4: Training must be provided to the satisfaction of the competent authority to enable hunters to become trained per- sons. It should cover at least the following subjects:

(a) the normal anatomy, physiology and behaviour of wild game;

(b) abnormal behaviour and pathological changes in wild game due to diseases, environmental contamination or other factors which may affect human health after consumption;

(c) the hygiene rules and proper techniques for the handling, transportation, evisceration, etc. of wild game animals after killing;

and

(d) legislation and administrative provisions on the animal and public health and hygiene conditions governing the placing on the market of wild game.

5: The competent authority should encourage hunters' organisations to provide such training.

CHAPTER II: HANDLING OF LARGE WILD GAME

1: After killing, large wild game must have their stomachs and intestines removed as soon as possible and, if necessary, are bled.

2: The trained person must carry out an examination of the body, and of any viscera removed, to identify any characteristics that may indicate that the meat presents a health risk. The examination must take place as soon as possible after killing.

3: Meat of large wild game may be placed on the market only if the body is transported to a game-handling establishment as soon as possible after the examination referred to in point 2. The viscera must accompany the body as specified in point 4. The viscera must be identifiable as belonging to a given animal.

4: (a) If no abnormal characteristics are found during the examination referred to in point 2, no abnormal behaviour was observed before killing, and there is no suspicion of environmental contamination, the trained person must attach to the animal body a numbered declaration stating this. This declaration must also indicate the date, time and place of killing. In this case, the head and the viscera need not accompany the body, except in the case of species susceptible to Trichinosis (porcine animals, solipeds and others), whose head (except for tusks) and diaphragm must accompany the body. However, hunters must comply with any additional requirements imposed in the Member State where hunting takes place, in particular to permit the monitoring of certain residues and substances in accordance with Directive 96/23/EC;

(b) In other circumstances, the head (except for tusks, antlers and horns) and all the viscera except for the stomach and intestines must accompany the body. The trained person who carried out the examination must inform the competent authority of the abnormal characteristics, abnormal behaviour or suspicion of environmental contamination that prevented him or her from making a declaration in accordance with (a);

(c) If no trained person is available to carry out the examination referred to in point 2 in a particular case, the head (except for tusks, antlers and horns) and all the viscera except for the stomach and the intestines must accompany the body.

5: Chilling must begin within a reasonable period of time after killing and achieve a temperature throughout the meat of not more than 7 °C. Where climatic conditions so permit, active chilling is not necessary.

6: During transport to the game-handling establishment, heaping must be avoided.

7: Large wild game delivered to a game-handling establishment must be presented to the competent authority for inspection.

CHAPTER III: HANDLING OF SMALL WILD GAME

1: The trained person must carry out an examination to identify any characteristics that may indicate that the meat presents a health risk. The examination must take place as soon as possible after killing.

2: If abnormal characteristics are found during the examination, abnormal behaviour was observed before killing, or environmental contamination is suspected, the trained person must inform the competent authority.

3: Meat of small wild game may be placed on the market only if the body is transported to a game-handling establishment as soon as possible after the examination referred to in point 1.

4: Chilling must begin within a reasonable period of time of killing and achieve a temperature throughout the meat of not more than 4 °C. Where climatic conditions so permit, active chilling is not necessary.

5: Evisceration must be carried out, or completed, without undue delay upon arrival at the game -handling establishment, unless the competent authority permits otherwise.

6: Small wild game delivered to a game-handling establishment must be presented to the competent authority for inspection.

CHAPTER XI

FORESTRY AND DEER

Overview – Forestry Processes (Planning, Establishment, Maintenance, Inventory, Thinning, Harvesting) – Damaging Impacts from Deer – Reducing/Preventing Damage – Physical Protection – Habitat Management – Deer Control

FORESTRY IN IRELAND – AN OVERVIEW

Approximately 10% of the land area of the republic of Ireland or just under 700,000 hectares is currently managed for timber production. Of this, 445,374 hectares or approximately 65% is currently owned and managed by Coillte Teoranta (Irish Forestry Board). An analysis of the Coillte forest estate is set out below.

The remaining 35% (approximately 245,000 hectares) is mainly in private ownership, spread over approximately 14,000 woodland owners. In all cases, woodland plantations represent a substantial investment of time and money for the landowner.

Coillte currently offer sporting licences for deer hunting on a relatively low percentage of their total land bank and the designated annual cull by licensees and nominated stalkers represents approximately 20% of the total annual cull of wild deer. To the annual designated cull through sporting licences must be added the cull taken by Coillte's own field staff and through Coillte's own accompanied stalking activities. Nonetheless it is evident that the number of deer culled on land owned other than by Coillte is significant and the principle of containment of deer numbers and prevention of damage by deer is as relevant to private woodland owners and to the farming community as it is to Coillte Teoranta.

The gender balance in numbers of deer returned as shot in recent years, typically being approximately 50:50 male:female, also serves to illustrate an underlying problem, which is that where damage from deer is a serious issue, and where deer numbers must be controlled through organised culling, not enough female deer are being shot. As previously stated in this training manual, the number of male deer culled makes very little difference to local numbers; control of female deer is the key to overall control of numbers and where numbers are a problem, the only solution is to increase the female cull to at least two-thirds of the total cull. It is against this general background that we must consider the issue of deer damage in forest plantations.

Ireland has one of the lowest coverages of woodland in Europe. Under the government's strategic plan for the development of the forest industry, Growing for the Future (1996), it is intended that this area will be increased to 1.2 million hectares of forestry or at least 17% of land coverage through an annual afforestation programme with a target 20,000 hectares to be planted each year for the period 2001-2030. Almost all current afforestation programmes are being undertaken by the private sector.

Broadleaved woodlands represent approximately 20% of all Irish forests, of which only 20,000 hectares can be classified as "semi-natural". The bulk of Ireland's forests are therefore coniferous, and conifers continue to represent approximately 70% of trees currently planted. Sitka spruce *(Picea sitchensis)* represents some 50% of conifer species planted, with the remainder being diverse conifers.

Leaf   *Sitka spruce*   *Fruit*

Forest operations in Ireland and associated environmental protection are regulated by a number of Acts of the Oireachtas, in particular the 1946, 1956 and 1988 Forestry Acts, as well as by a number of European Union Council Directives. The Forest Service, as part of the Department of Agriculture & Food, is the national authority for forestry in this country. As well as determining national forestry policy, the Forest Service is responsible for encouraging the development of private forestry through forestry grant schemes.

The concept of Sustainable Forest Management (SFM) aims to ensure that forests are managed in a sustainable manner, having regard for economic, environmental and social aspects. The Forest Management Standards for the Republic of Ireland – Draft, establishes specific criteria which need to be satisfied to ensure that forests are managed in accordance with the principles of SFM. Independent validation of compliance with these criteria is required in order that certification can be obtained. In May 2001, Coillte satisfied the Forest Stewardship Council's (FSC) certification process, confirming that their forests are managed in accordance with the principles of SFM, with consequent FSC certification. Other private forestry companies have also satisfied FSC certification requirements.

The Irish forest industry is hugely important for the national economy with an annual output now in excess of €500MN. It is estimated that nearly 10,000 people are currently employed either directly or indirectly in the forestry industry. Much of this employment is created in rural areas.

THE COILLTE FOREST ESTATE, 2004

The breakdown of the Coillte forest estate by land use categories and by species groups is set out below:

Land Use Categories	Gross Area (ha)
Area Forested	386,651
Area Felled/Blown etc.	14,733
Bare Land/Water/Swamp/Mountain etc.	43,990
Total Area Estate	**445,374**

Species Groups	Gross Area (ha)
Sitka spruce	251,514
Norway spruce	19,238
Pines	61,279
Other conifers	32,753
Broadleaves	21,867
Total	**386,651**

Source: Coillte Inventory Section, November 2004

FORESTRY PROCESSES

Planning

Managing a forest is a long-term process and is subject to a wide range of influences. All forest enterprises require careful planning in order to anticipate and manage operational, production and environmental policies and objectives.

Establishment

With the exception of sites where restocking is to be achieved through natural regeneration such as with continuous forest cover forestry, most forestry operations begin with the planting of a new, previously unplanted site (afforestation) or the replanting of a harvested site (reforestation).

Site development plans are produced for all establishment sites. These plans clearly detail the proposed layout and design of the site, ground preparation, drainage and fencing requirements as well as the selection of appropriate tree species, having regard for the following:

- Management objectives – including maximising timber volume in commercial forestry, broadleaf timber production, nature conservation in biodiversity sites
- Site conditions - soil type, fertility, altitude, aspect, drainage, etc.
- Access - roads, ridelines, firelines, etc.
- Landscape design plans
- Watercourses, archaeological sites, special features, biodiversity areas, power lines, etc.
- Certification Standard Requirements
- Compliance with Forest Service guidelines and code of best forest practice
- Compliance with felling licence requirements

Ground preparation prior to planting depends greatly on specific site conditions and generally involves the clearance of heavy ground vegetation, windrowing of brash (branches and other waste from harvesting operations), site drainage where necessary, the erection of perimeter fencing, and cultivation.

Most planting programmes are undertaken during the winter and spring months when the plants are dormant, however the use of plants from nurseries with specialist cold store facilities has extended the planting season late into the Spring. Although some mechanised planting is undertaken, most planting is still done by hand.

Maintenance

Once planted, the forest crop and site requires ongoing maintenance operations to ensure establishment. This may include:

- Replanting or filling in, which means replacing trees that have failed during the first few years immediately following planting. It is important that the cause of failure is identified and rectified.
- Weed Control - Hand weeding or chemical control (herbicide)
- Fertiliser application on infertile sites
- Protection from pests and diseases.
- Road construction and maintenance.
- Drain and fence maintenance.
- Brashing, path cutting and pruning
- Maintenance of biodiversity, conservation and amenity areas.
- Fire Protection and forest security.

Inventory

With respect to Coillte forest properties, inventory information relating to the forest crop is generally recorded at year 4 and again at year 14. This allows the crop's performance to be monitored, its yield assessed and production forecasts to be made, and it facilitates the planning and programming of thinning and harvesting operations. The Forest Service is currently undertaking an inventory of all woodland plantations, which commenced in 2004 and is due for completion in 2007.

Harvesting

Harvesting/felling is controlled by the issue of a general or limited felling licence by the Forest Service under the Forestry Act 1946.

Most harvesting and extraction methods are now highly mechanised and are undertaken as either thinning or final harvesting operations:

Thinning

Is the selective felling and removal of some of the tree crop to allow increased growth in timber volume of the remaining higher quality more vigorous trees. Most crops benefit from thinning and up to five thinnings can be undertaken on most crops. However with certain site conditions or the current state of certain forest crops, thinning operations are not undertaken.

In conifers, the first thinning generally takes place a few years after canopy closure when a top height of approximately 10 metres is reached. The timber harvested from thinning operations is generally saleable as pulp, pallet or stake material.

Final Harvesting

Harvesting the mature trees is the final operation of a forest's rotation. It is the usual practice in Ireland to clear-fell or remove all conifer trees from a harvesting site. Any broadleaf trees growing on the site are left unharvested as their rotation is much longer than that for conifers.

Red stags in coniferous forest.
The potential for damage is significant

The forest cycle commences again with the reforestation of the clear-fell site, which is a condition of the felling licence.

Damaging Impacts from deer

By damaging trees, wild deer can have a significant negative impact on forestry in Ireland.

In commercial forests, economic losses can be considerable, either as a direct result of the damage itself, or indirectly, from the high cost of crop protection, deer control and/or from having to select more damage-tolerant, less profitable crops rather than higher yielding, more valuable species.

In woodland areas managed primarily for nature conservation, biodiversity and amenity use, damaging impacts from wild deer can significantly reduce habitat values, prevent natural regeneration, and limit plant and animal diversity. Browsing impacts from deer can prevent the successful management of continuous cover forestry.

Deer damage forest crops in a number of ways:

Browsing

Browsing damage by deer in a forestry context generally refers to all forms of feeding damage other than bark stripping and thus includes the removal of buds, flowers, shoots, twigs leaves or needles from trees and the uprooting of small plants and seedlings.

The browsing of lateral buds or shoots, especially on trees greater than two metres in height, may have little actual impact on the growth of the tree itself. However browsing damage to terminal buds and leading shoots can severely check or stunt tree growth rates, and make them vulnerable to further browsing pressure for many years. In severe cases mortality of individual trees can result, although this is rare.

Severe deer browse damage to young broadleaf plant

In addition, the removal of the leading shoot greatly affects the tree's shape and form. In response, a number of lateral branches often compete to replace the leading shoot, resulting in "multi-leader" and misshapen trees developing. Such trees have little or no market value.

Deer are selective feeders. The parts of the tree browsed tend to depend on the trees species and the time of the year. Browsing is particularly prevalent in the months of January – May. Conifers usually tend to be browsed during the late winter when alternative food is scarce, whereas broadleaves are more often browsed during the spring and summer when buds and growing tips are most tender.

All deer species in Ireland can be responsible for causing browsing damage. However, certain tree species and plant heights tend to be more attractive to different deer species than others. Fallow deer, for example, tend to select the more palatable broadleaved tree species and softer conifers including Norway spruce (Picea abies), Scots pine (Pinus

Sika hind browsing

sylvestris), Douglas fir (Pseudotsuga menziesii) and larches (Larix Spp), with browsing of leading shoots on trees generally less than 1.4 metres in height. Nearly all tree species including Sitka spruce (Picea sitchensis) are vulnerable to the effects of browsing by sika and red deer. Where red deer are present, damage to leading shoots of trees in excess of 1.6 metres in height may result.

Douglas fir

Leaf and cone

Being more subtle and less obvious than the other forms of damage, browsing and its effects may go generally unnoticed during the early years of a crop's establishment. However long-term economic effects can be considerable.

In forest sites suitable for natural regeneration, browsing pressure from deer can totally suppress that natural regeneration. By reducing or removing the forest's understory and shrub layers, browsing by deer can restrict plant and structural diversity and greatly reduce the biodiversity value of the woodland habitat.

Severe deer damage on replanted hillside

Fraying

Fraying, also referred to as "rubbing" or "trashing", is damage caused to trees, particularly the bark, side branches and foliage, by the rubbing of antlers and/or

Sheep will also cause measurable damage in young plantations

facial scent glands up and down the tree stem. This activity is generally associated with the removal of velvet from antlers and during pre-rut scent marking and therefore mainly occurs during the months of August – November. On young trees, aggressive fraying can prove fatal for the affected tree by removing the bark or breaking or severely damaging the stem.

All deer species in Ireland can be responsible for causing fraying damage, but it is particularly evident with fallow and red deer. The availability of suitable tree stems is perhaps more important to the deer than the actual species of tree itself.

Although it can be perhaps one of the most obvious forms of deer damage in forestry, fraying tends to be restricted to individual trees and its effects on the forest crop, although generally limited, may be severe in extreme cases.

Fraying damage on a young Sitka spruce tree

Severe fraying damage, involving a red deer stag in woodland

Bark stripping

Bark stripping or "peeling" is the removal and eating of the bark from the tree by deer. This is generally done using the lower incisor teeth in an upward direction. Where the bark is easily removed, loose strands of bark are often left hanging on the stem to the upper side of the wound. Visible tooth marks are often apparent on the wound; the width of these marks combined with the overall height of the wound may indicate the species of deer responsible. Bark stripping generally occurs to the main stem of the tree, however it can also occur to side branches and root buttresses. Although fresh stripping is generally fairly obvious in pre-thicket crops or at the edge of forest road or ride lines, it can continue unnoticed in thicket stage compartments.

Although all deer species in Ireland can be responsible for stripping bark from trees, on upland forest sites it tends to be least associated with fallow deer and most common in areas where red, sika and red/sika hybrid animals are present. However bark-stripping damage on lowland sites is often attributable to fallow deer. Damage is usually greatest in large upland conifer plantations. It has been extreme in some cases, particularily in broadleaf trees in some midland counties.

Many broadleaves tree species can be affected, however currently its effects are greatest felt in the large upland conifer plantations of Sitka spruce *(Picea sitchensis)*, Norway spruce *(Picea abies)*, Scots pine *(Pinus sylvestris)*, larch *(Larix Spp)*, Douglas fir *(Pseudotsuga menziesii)*, and Lodgepole pine *(Pinus contorta)*. In areas of Co. Wicklow, damage levels in excess of 65% have frequently been recorded in crops of Sitka spruce less than 15 years of age.

Lodgepole pine

Needles and fruit

The tree's susceptibility to bark stripping is generally related to age and size, with damage beginning shortly after planting when the stem becomes rigid and ends when the bark becomes too coarse and difficult to remove. Experience with Sitka spruce in Co. Wicklow indicates that peak levels occur between 4 – 9 years, with few outbreaks being recorded after year 20.

Severe bark stripping damage

The occurrence of bark stripping is extremely variable between areas and between years. It can occur in a constant rate of a few trees every year or suddenly as an outbreak every few years. Although bark stripping can occur during the winter in some areas, it is generally during the spring months when it is most evident, often re-occurring in late summer and early autumn.

Bark stripping can have enormous economic consequences for the forest industry. Peeling wounds, extending completely around the stem, will kill the tree. With other wounds, the removal of bark permits fungal infection of the stem causing rot and staining to the timber, and causes concentric growth patterns as the tree endeavours to grow over and to cover the wound. This weakens many stems causing them to break in subsequent years, or if they survive to be harvested, will ensure that they will not satisfy the appropriate standards and will be downgraded to a less valuable product.

Much bark stripping can be found deep in a forest plantation where there is little other feeding for deer

At felling: The effect of bark stripping on timber growth

Bole Scoring

Bole scoring is generally associated with sika and sika-like hybrid deer, however it does not commonly occur in Ireland. Damage is caused when male deer using antler points (tines) dig deep vertical gouges or scores in the bark of mature trees during the rut period between late September and late November. Smooth-barked trees species appear to be more vulnerable than those with coarse bark.

Bole scoring by a sika stag on a larch tree

Reducing / Preventing damaging impacts

Strategies aimed at reducing / preventing damaging impacts of deer generally consist of a combination of three different management options:

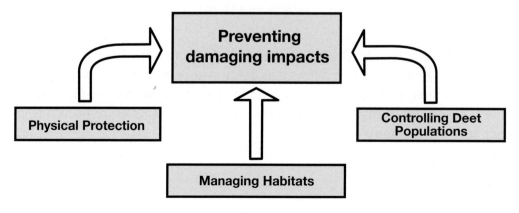

Physical Protection

The physical protection of trees generally involves the erection of protective deer fencing or the use of individual tree guards or shelters. Such methods are generally regarded as providing effective protection to small areas of highly vulnerable crops or individual trees.

Managing Habitats

In forest areas where the presence of wild deer is considered likely to compromise the future management objectives of the forest area by damaging crops, serious consideration must be given to the tree species selected as well as incorporating layout and design techniques which provide the deer with alternative food (other than the tree crop) and facilitates deer management and control at all stages of a crop's rotation.

Controlling Deer Populations

The control of deer numbers at densities appropriate to their environment and the vulnerability of the forest crop is generally regarded as the most effective, long-term strategy for reducing / preventing the damaging effects of wild deer.

Lough Tay at Luggala, near Roundwood, Co. Wicklow - home to a significant population of sika deer

CHAPTER XII

IMPACTS OF DEER ON NATURE CONSERVATION HABITATS

National Heritage Areas – Special Areas of Conservation – Special Protection Areas – Grazing, Sporting and Turf-Cutting Rights – Conservation Planning

When we consider impact by deer species we traditionally think of their impact on commercial forestry or agriculture.

The density of deer (and other grazers) has an effect on the plant species present in a particular habitat. While low levels of grazing may have little effect on species succession, higher levels may halt succession completely and may cause habitat degradation. All Irish woodlands have evolved in the presence of deer and other grazers. Deer play an important role in creating diverse structures, which favour many plant and animal species. Grazed oakwood specialist species such as redstart (Phoenicurus phoenicurus), wood warber (Phylloscopus sibilatrix) and pied flycatcher (Ficedula hypoleuca) require a level of grazing which prevents the domination of certain ground vegetation (Smart & Andrews 1985). Ratcliffe (1997) found that red deer densities higher than 10 deer /100ha can reduce botanical diversity. Very high densities can cause a change in heather moorland to acid grassland. Densities higher than 4 - 8 deer / 100ha can prevent growth of trees. For successful natural regeneration of native broadleaf species to occur densities as low as 2 deer /100ha should generally not be exceeded. In the case of Creagh Meagaidh National Nature Reserve in Scotland, deer densities were reduced from 19 to less than 5 deer /100ha. This resulted in an increase in natural regeneration of Willow (Salix spp.), Birch (Betula pubescens), and Rowan (Sorbus aucuparius) from less than 50 seedlings in 1990/91 to over 3,700 in 1995/96 (Ramsay,1996).

However unlike damage to trees and commercial forestry, changes and damage to other habitats may be less apparent and take place over a long time period. Only in severe cases is it obvious, at lower levels it may only change species composition, possibly resulting in the loss of rare and sensitive species.

As a result of European and national legislation we are legally obliged to protect a wide range of conservation habitats and species. As a result not just in Ireland, but across Europe, an area the size of Germany has been designated under European law to protect rare habitats & species. We are all obliged to "maintain and enhance" the conservation interests of these sites. This means the prevention/prohibition of damaging activities within these sites, most of these are direct human impacts which are obvious enough, land drainage, land clearance, unauthorised developments etc. But there are also ecological impacts, which cause an imbalance in our natural systems, the introduction of exotic species, which in the absence of predators and diseases out compete our native plant and animal species. This may have the effect of destroying or changing habitats and the loss of species we are trying to protect. This can be clearly seen in the case of the introduced rhododendron into oak woodlands particularly in the Killarney area. The impacts on these habitats by deer and other grazers may also need to be addressed. With the exception of red deer in Killarney, we are dealing with introduced species, and none are protected under the Habitats Directive. Outside of the designated areas in the general countryside we are also obliged to maintain bio-diversity as outlined in the National Bio-diversity Plan.

Types of Conservation Site Designation

The three main types of designation are
- 'Natural Heritage Area', or NHA
- 'Special Area of Conservation', or SAC
- 'Special Protection Area', or SPA

The majority of this land is in private ownership, some are in State ownership and includes terrestrial and marine sites. The State-owned sites include national parks, State nature reserves, marine areas below the high tide line, and State owned lakes.

NHAs – Natural Heritage Areas

The basic designation for wildlife is the Natural Heritage Area. In 1995, proposals for over 1,100 NHAs were published, but it was not until December 2000 that powers were introduced for the statutory process of their designation and protection. Many of these NHAs have overlapping designations of SAC and/or SPA. There are currently 802 proposed NHAs which are not SAC/SPA. They cover an area of about 113,000 hectares. These will be reviewed, and other sites surveyed, during the course of the designation process. Some of the proposed As (pNHAs) are tiny, such as a roosting place for rare bats. Others are large – for example, a blanket bog or a lake.

The Geological Survey of Ireland (GSI) is compiling a list of geological sites in need of protection through NHA designation. A committee of expert geologists chooses the sites. These will be designated over a period of time, with the most "at risk" sites receiving protection first. The GSI has completed its list of karst (i.e. exposed limestone) and early fossil sites. The process of formal designation of NHAs has now commenced. It is hoped that most landowners will appreciate the need for protection of wildlife areas and will be satisfied with the incentives and compensation available. However, it will be possible for the landowner to object on scientific grounds to a proposed designation if he or she wishes, before the designation is confirmed. After allowing time for landowners to consider and if necessary appeal the proposed areas, the Minister will formally designate these sites.

Prior to statutory designation, proposed NHAs are subject to limited protection, in the form of:

- Rural Environment Protection Scheme (REPS) plans which require conservation of NHAs and operate for a period of 5 years.

- Ineligibility of NHA lands for certain grants, in particular for Forestry grants

- Recognition of NHA values by Planning and Licencing Authorities.

Under the Wildlife Amendment Act (2000), NHAs are legally protected from damage from the date they are formally proposed.

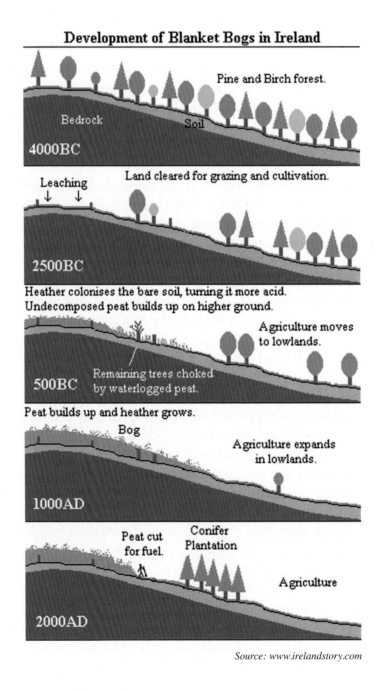

Source: www.irelandstory.com

SACs – Special Areas of Conservation

These are prime wildlife conservation areas in the country, considered to be important at European level as well as at national level. They are chosen from the pNHAs, although a number of known high quality sites which are not yet NHAs have also been included. Most SACs are in the countryside, although a few sites reach into town or city landscapes, such as Dublin Bay and Cork Harbour. The legal basis on which SACs are selected and designated is the EU Habitats Directive (92/43/EEC), transposed into Irish law in the European Union (Natural Habitats) Regulations, 1997. The directive lists certain habitats and species that must be given protection in SACs. Irish habitats include raised bogs, active blanket bogs, turloughs, sand dunes, machair (flat sandy plains on the north and west coasts), heaths, lakes, rivers, woodlands, estuaries, and sea inlets. The 25 Irish species which must be afforded protection include salmon, otter, freshwater pearl mussel, Bottle-nosed dolphin and Killarney Fern. Some habitats are deemed "priority" and have greater requirements for designation of sites and protection. Sites that meet criteria laid down by the EU Directive are identified by National Parks & Wildlife Service and proposed for designation. To date, Ireland has transmitted 420 sites to the European Commission as special areas of conservation.

These cover an area of approximately 10,000 square kilometres. Across the EU, over 12,600 sites have been identified and proposed, covering an area of 420,000 sq. km.

SPAs - Special Protection Areas

These sites are areas of importance to birds (and often are important for other types of wildlife).The EU Birds Directive (79/409/EEC) requires designation of SPAs for:

- Listed rare and vulnerable species such as whooper swan, Greenland white-fronted goose, peregrine falcon, corncrake and terns.

- Regularly occurring migratory species, such as ducks, geese and waders.

- Wetlands, especially those of international importance, which attract large numbers of migratory birds each year. ("internationally important" means that 1% of the population of a species uses the site, or more than 20,000 birds regularly use the site.)

Some of the listed species conveniently occur in high numbers and densities. However, others such as breeding waders and birds of prey, occur at very low density where designation of sites is a more difficult, although necessary, exercise. To date, 110 SPAs have been designated. A further 25 sites have been notified to landowners. Approximately 25 SPAs are also designated SAC. The Irish SPAs join a total of around 3,000 sites across the European Union.

Special Areas of Conservation and Special Protection Areas collectively form part of 'Natura 2000', a network of protected areas throughout the European Union. Across the EU, sites forming part of 'Natura 2000' cover an area of land and sea the size of Germany.

Grazing, Sporting and Turf-Cutting Rights

Those who own these rights have the same responsibility as landowners to ensure that their activities do not damage the wildlife quality of a site. Any person who illegally damages a site may be prosecuted or required to repair damage. The designation of a SAC, SPA or NHA rarely affects the shooting interests on the site.

Conservation Planning

National Parks & Wildlife Service are obliged to produce a draft conservation plan for each SAC, SPA and NHA. A plan will list the wildlife resources of the area, the current human uses, any conflicts between the two, and strategies for retaining the conservation value. This draft document will be given to the liaison committee (comprising of landowners and right holders) and other interested parties for discussion and consultation. National Parks & Wildlife Service will then prepare a final version of the conservation plan. Consultation on plans began in 2001. Plans will be reviewed on a 5-year cycle. It is at this stage the issues that may impact or are impacting on a site are outlined, for instance over grazing of oak woodland by deer. In the plan strategies will be outlined to protect the site e.g. in the case of overgrazing by deer by reducing the density of animals present either by increased culling or fencing. National Parks & Wildlife Service are also obliged to monitor the conservation status of these sites on at least a 3 year cycle with a report being made to the EU every 6 years.

A useful publication which gives an overview of these Designations and the processes of designation are outlined in "Living with Nature" available free from National Parks & Wildlife Service.

National Parks & Wildlife Service has a network of local conservation rangers located across Ireland. They can discuss queries in relation to nature conservation issues affecting lands in their areas. For Conservation Ranger contact details, please see: *http://www.npws.ie/en/NPWSStaffOrganisation/RegionalManagement/d6790.en.v1.0.t4. DOC*

Further information on conservation sites is also available from:

> **Helpline:** 1800-405000
> (calls to this line are free from within the Republic of Ireland)
> **Fax:** 01-6620283
> (please mark for the attention of
> NPWS Site Designations & Plans Unit)
> **e-mail:** natureconservation@environ.ie
> **web:** www.environ.ie or www.npws.ie
> **GIS web:** www.heritagedata.ie
> **Postal address:** National Parks & Wildlife Service, 7 Ely Place, Dublin 2.

APPENDICES

APPENDIX I

CURRENT OPEN SEASONS FOR WILD DEER
(REPUBLIC OF IRELAND)

THE FOLLOWING OPEN SEASONS FOR WILD DEER INTRODUCED UNDER THE PROVISIONS OF THE WILDLIFE (WILD MAMMALS) (OPEN SEASONS) ORDER, 2005 AND REMAIN IN FORCE AT TIME OF PUBLICATION.

FOR LATEST NEWS AND INFORMATION CONTACT THE WILDLIFE SERVICE OR REFER TO THE DEER ALLIANCE WEBSITE OR INTERNET BLOG (www.deeralliance.ie or www.deeralliance.blogspot.com)

SPECIES	OPEN SEASON DATES	LOCATION
Red Deer Male	1 September to 31 December	Throughout the State exclusive of the County of Kerry
Red Deer Female and Antlerless Deer*	1 November to 28 February	Throughout the State
Sika Deer Male	1 September to 31 December	Throughout the State
Sika Deer Female and Antlerless Deer*	1 November to 28 February	Throughout the State
Fallow Deer Male	31 December 1 September to	Throughout the State
Fallow Deer Female and Antlerless Deer*	1 November to 28 February	Throughout the State

* Antlerless deer will be construed as including any male deer without antlers,
of less than one year, i.e. a calf.
The ordinary period for which a deer hunting licence may be granted is from date of issue to
the following July 31
A limited Open Season for Muntjac deer was introduced in 2008,ending on 28 February 2008.
For current information on the status of Muntjac deer,
contact the Wildlife Service or refer to the Deer Alliance website.

APPENDIX II

APPLYING FOR A LICENCE TO HUNT DEER

Licences to hunt deer are granted by the Minister under section 29 of the Wildlife Act, 1976 (as amended). Applications are made to the National Parks & Wildlife Service at 7 Ely Place, Dublin 2 (Telephone No. 01-647 3000, Lo-Call: 1890-321 421, Fax: 01 662 0283) from whom applications forms are available.

Applicants must provide:

- name
- address
- contact telephone number
- date of birth
- details of ground over which it is proposed to hunt (county, townland, area in acres or hectares, name and address of owner or occupier and name and address of person entitled to sporting rights over the lands in question, and Land Registry folio number of the lands
- original and current letter of permission to hunt over the land, signed by the landowner, occupier and/or person entitled to the sporting rights. In the case of an application based on a permit issued by Coillte Teoranta, a photocopy of the permit is acceptable
- details of firearm to be used, including maker's name, calibre, serial number and bullet weight
- details of whether any previous licence has been held by the applicant
- details of any deer shot by the applicant in the previous season (location where shot, species, number)

The application form must be signed and dated by the applicant and the applicant's signature must be witnessed, and witness's address provided.

There is currently no fee imposed on the issue of a licence to hunt deer.

The application should be forwarded to National Parks & Wildlife Service at 7 Ely Place, Dublin 2.

If a first-time application, National Parks & Wildlife Service, as the licensing authority, will normally remit the application to the local Conservation Ranger in the area concerned for verification before issue of licence.

Applications for second or subsequent licences will normally be invited by National Parks & Wildlife Service between May – July each year. Period of validity will be shown on the licence but normally runs from date of issue to the following 31st day of July.

APPENDIX III

'SECTION 42' LICENCE APPLICATIONS

Section 42 of the Wildlife Act, 1976 (as amended) provides for the control of protected wild birds and animals where they are causing serious damage to:

- Food, livestock, poultry or crops, either on pasture or on cultivated lands.
- Pen-reared wild birds
- Other fauna
- Flora
- Woodland or forestry plantation
- Any Fishery
- Buildings and other structures and their contents
- Aquaculture installations

The Minister may authorise on his behalf any person to take such steps as to stop the damage, inside or outside any Open Season, if applicable. This can include entering any land and scaring, capturing or killing any protected wild bird or animal, as appropriate to stop the damage.

In practical terms this control takes the form of a licence issued to the landowner, agent or nominee.

Applications for 'Section 42' licences are made on a standard application form available from National Parks & Wildlife Service local offices or from National Parks & Wildlife Service Head Office (Licensing Section) at 6 Ely Place, Dublin 2.

This application must be completed in full as follows:

Name of applicant: The name of the person who is experiencing the damage (normally the landowner)

Address: address to which all correspondence is to be sent, normally the applicant's home address.

Telephone number: contact number for applicant (to assist field staff in making a speedy site inspection and recommendation)

Species causing the damage: in this case 'deer' but if the species is known it should be included e.g. sika, fallow or red etc.

Particulars of damage: Detail of the damage being caused e.g. bark stripping of trees, damage to spring cereals etc.

Location where damage is occurring: address, if different to applicant's address.

State whether it is proposed to capture, scare or kill the species in question: in general in the case of deer it is to kill but sometimes applicants may wish to scare only, so as to discourage their presence. Capture of the species in question normally only occurs with smaller species that become trapped in a building, for example, a Pine Marten.

Proposed means of capture or killing: in the case of deer species this normally refers to a rifle of a calibre legal for killing wild deer i.e. minimum .22/250 calibre with 55 grain bullet. In the case of scaring only, it may be a shotgun. Reference should be made also to any other special requirements e.g. use of a lamp.

Method of disposal: Normally for deer, this will either be 'home consumption' or 'sale to a licensed Wildlife Dealer'. Applicants should note the issue of this licence does not free them from other legal obligations arising other legislation, e.g. Environmental Health Acts or Department of Agriculture Regulations e.g. if (for instance) the animals are to be disposed of by burial.

Period for which permission is required: This refers to the period for which the applicant requires the licence. In practice, National Parks & Wildlife Service field staff will generally recommend issue for a period of **from four to six weeks** as a maximum, subject to review at that time and, if necessary, a possible recommendation to extend.

Nominated stalker: If the applicant does not have the necessary time, skills or equipment to execute the licence they may nominate someone else to do it.

Date of application: Date on which application is made.

Signature of Applicant: normally the application must be signed by the landowner unless the applicant is specifically requested in writing to make the application on behalf of the landowner as necessary.

Completed applications to be returned to the local office of National Parks & Wildlife Service or to National Parks & Wildlife Service Head Office at 7 Ely Place, Dublin 2.

NOTE: Licences are issued with standard condition attached but additional conditions may be imposed by the Minister as appropriate or necessary.

The licence will usually stipulate the maximum number of deer to be killed, often specifying sex.

A return of all species captured or killed must be sent to National Parks & Wildlife Service at the end of the licence period.

APPENDIX IV

COILLTE TEORANTA LICENCE
(Subject to amendment)

SPORTING LICENCE

SPECIMEN

FOR THE HUNTING OF WILD DEER ON FOREST PROPERTY

Revised 22 July 2002

coillte

Memorandum of Agreement

Licence Number: - _____

Forest: - _____

Properties included: - _____

_____

_____

_____

Annual Licence Fee _____ (Not inclusive of VAT)

Licence Commencement Date: - ____/____/____

Licence Expiry Date: - ____/____/____

I, _____ of _____

_____ agree to the Terms and Conditions attached to this Deer Stalking Licence for the aforementioned lands owned by Coillte Teo;

SIGNED _____ **DATE** ____/____/____

coillte

coillte

This Licence (Number _____) made the _____ day of _____

_____ between **COILLTE TEORANTA** having its registered office at Leeson Lane,

Leeson Street, Dublin 2 (hereinafter called "the Licensor") of the one part

and _____

of _____

_____

_____

(hereinafter called " the Licensee" which expression shall where the context so admits or requires include all holders of annual permits as hereinafter defined) of the other part

WHEREBY it is agreed as follows:-

1.   The Licensor hereby grants unto the Licensee the licence and authority to enter upon the lands specified in the First Schedule hereto (hereinafter called "the Lands" during and for the period specified in the Second Schedule hereto for the use only specified in the the Third Schedule hereto and subject to the terms and Conditions herein set forth and to the Special Conditions (if any) set out in the Fourth Schedule hereto.

2.   (i) Neither the Licensee nor any person on its behalf shall be entitled to exercise the rights conferred by this Agreement without an individual permit (hereinafter called an annual stalking permit) granted by the licensor each year during the period of this Licence.

(ii) The Licensee, not later than 3 months before the commencement of each stalking season shall make application to the Licensor for the granting of annual stalking permits to the persons named therein. This application shall be accompanied by evidence that the said persons carry such insurance cover as may be required by the licensor pursuant to Clause 10 hereof for the duration of the deer stalking season.

(iii) The Licensor shall grant annual stalking permits at its sole discretion but only if satisfied that the persons in respect of whom application is made are suitable to exercise the rights conferred by this Agreement and may also require that such persons demonstrate their competence by successfully completing a nationally recognised competence test.

(iv) The Licensor shall issue each successful applicant with a permit subject to the terms and conditions of this agreement and this permit must be carried by its holder whenever exercising his rights under this agreement and produced on request to the Licensor, its employees, servants or agents or to members of the Garda Siochana, or persons appointed by the Minister for the Environment and Local Government under Sec (72) of The Wildlife Act 1976 (as amended) To be an authorised person for the purposes of that Act .

(v) The annual stalking permits granted by the Licensor under this Agreement shall not exceed the number specified in the Fourth Schedule hereto.

3.   The Licensor and the Licensee shall appoint the persons named in the Fourth Schedule hereto liase with each other on all matters pertaining to these agreement.

4.   **The Licensee AGREES with the Licensor as follows: -**

    a.   To pay the licence fees specified in the Fourth Schedule.

    b.   To use the lands solely for the purposes specified in the Third Schedule hereto.

    c.   To comply in all respects with the annual deer cull programme furnished by the licensor to the Licensee to the intent that the Licensee shall cull only the quantity and sex of deer stipulated in the cull programme (Fourth Schedule (7)).

          To affix identity tags, supplied by the licensor, to the carcass of any culled deer, prior to their removal from the licensed area.

    d.   To furnish accurate mid-season and end of season cull data in a format to be prescribed by the Licensor.

    e.   To assist any on going scientific research of the Licensor by furnishing detailed information relating to the animals culled (including samples for analysis) and field observations of the animals in the wild.

    f.   Not to attempt to deal with or dispose of the rights granted hereunto which are purely personal to the Licensee otherwise than is hereinafter provided.

    g.   To give the Forester-in-charge 48 hours notice of its intention to exercise its rights under this agreement. The notice shall contain particulars of all permit holders intending to stalk at that time.

    h.   To post notices in a format to be approved by the Licensor at all entrances to the lands prior to commencement of stalking and to remove same on cessation of stalking.

i. Not to exercise its rights along any forest roads, public pathways or in the vicinity of any residence or buildings.

j. To exercise the rights of stalking and culling deer in a proper and sportsmanlike manner and in accordance with all current wildlife legislation.

k. Not to cause nuisance to, annoyance or damage to the Licensor's property, stock, fences, gates or any other property or interfere in any way with the Licensor's undertaking on or use of the lands or disturb, damage or interfere with or move any of the flora, fauna, wildlife, game (other than deer) or other natural phenomena on the lands.

l. To keep the lands clean, tidy and in good order and to pay for any damage thereto or expense of clearing the same caused by any damage.

m. Not to light fires on the land.

n. To close all gates and take such reasonable steps as may be necessary to protect the lands.

o. To make good or pay the costs of making good any damage to the Licensor's property (including damage to roads, drains, fences, gates or stiles arising out of the exercise of the licence).

p. On termination of the Licence, to remove at its own expense from the Licensor's lands any structure or installation which may have been placed thereon by it and restore the ground to its original condition to the Licensor's satisfaction

q. To use only a licensed firearm of approved calibre.

r. Not to duplicate any keys issued by the licensor and to return such keys on the termination / expiration of the licence.

s. Not to dispose of any viscera or other carcass waste on the lands.

t. To notify the relevant authorities of any abnormal conditions or suspected diseases observed in the culled animals.

u. If requested by the licensor to provide a written deer management strategy or to assist in the development of a similar deer management plan for the licensed area and to meet with the licensor to discuss the implementation of such a plan.

v. To determine the boundaries of the licensed area in consultation with the forest manager.

5. Annual permit holders shall not be entitled to exercise rights under this agreement unless in possession of a current Deer Hunting Licence issued by Dúchas/ National Parks & Wildlife Service, in accordance with the provisions of The *Wildlife Act 1976 (as amended)* and shall furnish evidence of same whenever requested to do so by the Licensor, its servants, agents or employees.

6. **(i)** The licensor may, by notice in writing to the Licensee, add to or vary the conditions and obligations contained under the Agreement from time to time as it may consider reasonable for the protection of its property and the good management of the lands.

(ii) Notwithstanding this Agreement the Licensor reserves the right to control (and shoot) deer and other species on the lands if it is considered necessary for the good management thereof.

7. **i)** The Licensor's use and enjoyment of its property of which the lands form part and all its undertakings on its property whether carried on by it or persons authorised directly or indirectly by it, shall take precedence over the use authorised by this licence and the licensee shall not be entitled to exclusive possession or occupation for any purpose of the lands or any part of them or be entitled to make any claim to or for compensation in respect of interference with its use thereof.

ii) The Licensor may from time to time prohibit at its absolute discretion, the activities permitted under this Licence or the use of any part of the lands to which the Licence applies as it may specify in writing to the Licensee **PROVIDED ALWAYS** that the Licensor shall notify the Licensee of any restriction under this part of the agreement as soon as the Licensee shall notify the Licensor of its intention to exercise its rights under the agreement under clause 4 (g) thereof.

8. **i)** The Licensor may terminate this Licence without prejudice to claim which it may have against the Licensee in respect of breach of any of the provisions of the Licence: -

ii) By not less than one months notice in writing to expire on the date specified in the notice.

iii) At any time by written notice to the Licensee's nominee in the event of serious breach of any of the conditions of this agreement or in the event of wilful or unnecessary damage to the Licensor's property.

9. The Licensee shall not be entitled to any compensation from the Licensor for disturbance of for any loss or damage nor shall the licensee be entitled to enter upon the lands or any portion thereof upon or after termination of these presents and the Licensee **hereby acknowledges** that this licence is granted subject to termination forthwith by the Licensor at any time at the Licensor's sole and absolute discretion.

10. **i)** The Licensee and any persons having resort to the lands by virtue of or in exercise or purported exercise of the privileges and rights conferred by this licence shall do so at their own risk in all respects and the licensor makes no representation or warranty as to suitability of the lands for the use specified in the Third Schedule hereto or for any use by the licensee howsoever arising.

ii) The Licensee and any persons having resort to the lands by virtue of or in exercise or purported exercise of the privileges and rights conferred by this Agreement shall indemnify and save harmless the Licensor from and against all actions arising out of injury to any person or los   s or damage to any property whatsoever resulting from or in any way connected with or arising out of the

Licence and shall further indemnify the Licensor it's employees and agents from liability in respect of any personal injury or damage to a property sustained by the Licensor or by its officers , employees or agents through or arising out of any act or omission of the Licensee or persons having resort to the lands by virtue of or in exercise or purported exercise of the privileges and rights conferred by these presents including indemnification for the Licensor from and against liability to its workmen under the Occupational Injuries Code if and whenever a claim under these acts shall arise from an act or omission by the Licensee or persons having resort to the said lands by virtue of in exercise or purported exercise of the privileges and rights conferred by these presents.

11. Without prejudice or limitation to the Licensee's liability the Licensee shall maintain the Insurance's set out hereunder and shall furnish evidence of same to the Licensor prior to commencement of this Licence and in subsequent years prior to the date specified in the Fourth Schedule, together with a receipt in respect of the payment of the Premium thereon: -

     (i) Membership of the National Association of Regional Game Councils Compensation fund .

     OR

     Public Liability Insurance with an indemnity of not less than €2,540,000.00 for any one accident to include an indemnity to the Licensor as joint Insured and to include cross-liabilities clause set out hereunder - "for the purpose of this Policy each of the parties comprising the Insured shall be considered a separate and distinct unit and the words 'the Insured' shall be considered as applying to each party in the same manner as if a separate Policy had been issued to each of the said parties and the Insurers hereby agree to waive all rights of subrogation or action which the Underwriters have or require against either of the aforesaid parties arising out of an accident in respect of any claims made hereunder".

     (ii) Motor Third Party Liability Insurance with a minimum of €1,270,000.00 third party property damage limit in respect of all vehicles used in connection with the Licence which will require to be insured under the provisions of the Road Traffic Acts with indemnity to the Licensor in respect of any liability that arises by reason of negligence of the Licensee or any person, servant or agent arising from the use of the motor vehicles.

12. Any notice required to be given by either party under the terms of this agreement shall (save as otherwise provided) be given by delivery by registered letter or facsimile (confirmed by registered letter) addressed to the party for whom it was intended at its last known address. Every notice shall be deemed to have been received and given at the time if delivered upon delivery and if sent by registered letter when in the ordinary course of transmission it should have been delivered to the address to which it was sent or within 72 hours after the date of such notice whichever is earlier.

FIRST SCHEDULE

Description of Lands
(see adjoining map)

REGION : _____

Forest :- _____

Property Code:- _____

Properties :- _____

_____

_____

_____

_____

SECOND SCHEDULE

Period of Licence

The Licence shall be for the hours between dawn and 11am for the period from the 1st day of September to the 28th day of February each year commencing on the _____ day of _____ and will expire on the _____ day of _____.

THIRD SCHEDULE

Us

The Licence is granted solely for the purpose of stalking and culling wild deer and the rights hereunder shall be exercised only during the declared shooting season as determined under current wildlife legislation and only during the hours between dawn and _____11 am.

On application written permission may be granted by the licensor to the licensee to allow evening shooting for the period of two hours before dusk. Such permission shall only be in respect of specifically approved sites and shall be restricted to shooting from "high seats" or
similar elevated shooting positions only. The licensee shall however indemnify and save harmless the Licensor from and against all actions arising out of injury to any person or loss or damage to any property whatsoever resulting from or in any way connected with or arising from the use of such "high seats" (in accordance with Clause 11 hereof).

FOURTH SCHEDULE

Special Conditions

1) Licence Fee: -

The Licensee shall pay an annual licence fee of _____together with VAT

at an appropriate rate. This Licence fee is to be paid prior to the 30th of June each year.

2) Evidence of insurance: -

The licensee shall provide, prior to the 30th of June each year, details relating to those persons nominated to exercise these rights. This application should be accompanied by evidence that the said persons carry such insurance cover as may be required by the licensor pursuant to clause 11 hereof.

3) Forester in charge: -

The current forester in charge of the properties to which this Licence relates is: -

Name: - _____ Tel number: - _____

4) Licensor's nominee: - _____

5) Licensee's nominee: - _____

6) Number of annual permits: -

The number of annual permits to be issued on each Licence will be at the discretion of the Licensor. The maximum number of permit holders should not exceed the annual cull figure.

7) The Annual Cull Programme: -

The number and sex of deer (cull programme) that the Licensee is permitted to cull under the Licence is determined annually.

8) Vehicle Access: -

Vehicle access to forestry property may be permitted at the discretion of the Licensor. This is for the recovery of carcasses only. Only road vehicles insured under the provisions of the Road Traffic Acts (in accordance with Clause 11 (ii) hereof) shall be permitted. The use of "all terrain vehicles" (A.T.V's) including "Quad bikes" is prohibited.

9) Trained Tracking Dogs: -

All persons intending to hunt deer on Coillte's property must have access to a trained tracking dog for the recovery and humane dispatch of any deer injured from shooting.

Additional conditions: -

9) _____

_____

_____

10) _____

_____

_____

Signed on behalf of the Licensor: -_____

Authorised   Signature

Official Stamp: -

coillte

APPENDIX V

PRESCRIBED FORMAT FOR WARNING SIGNS
ON COILLTE TEORANTA FOREST PROPERTY

MINIMUM SIZE 400 M.M. x 600 M.M.

APPENDIX VI

AGE ESTIMATION BY TOOTH WEAR

The teeth of deer, as with other animal species, erupt from the bone of the skull and lower jaw (mandible) in a regular fashion. Young deer can be accurately aged by checking which teeth have erupted, first with the eruption of the deciduous or milk teeth and then the permanent set. The premolar and molar teeth are used to grind down the fibrous plant tissue in the deer's diet to make it more available for bacterial digestion in the rumen.

The rate of wear of these teeth is a very good indication of age, though even for animals of the same species there is a variation in wear rate between different locations where the type of grazing or soil conditions vary.

The full complement of teeth for red and sika deer is as follows:

	Incisors	Canines	Premolars	Molars
Top Jaw	0	2	6	6
Lower Jaw	6	2	6	6

Fallow deer have no upper canine teeth so their dentition is as follows:

	Incisors	Canines	Premolars	Molars
Top Jaw	0	0	6	6
Lower Jaw	6	2	6	6

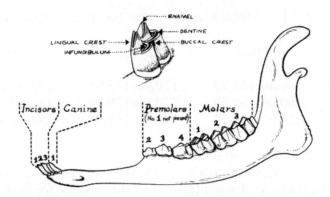

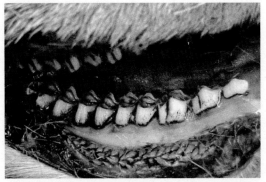

Known age 18 months: Temporary premolars present (fourth premolar is 3-parted). In deer, the first premolar is vestigial, not present, remaining premolars are the second, third and fourth

Known age three & one-half years: Last cusp of third molar flattened on the buccal crest. Dentine line on the last cusp is C or J shaped. Third premolar with thin to moderate dentine line on anterior surface. Lingual crest of first molar blunt. Lingual crests of other molars sharp

APPENDIX VII

TROPHY EVALUATION AND PREPARATION

The internationally accepted system for evaluation and scoring of deer heads is that of the Conseil International de la Chasse (C.I.C.), which covers our three Irish deer species. This system provides an estimation of the comparative excellence of the head on a world scale, with heads prepared and measured according to strict and consistent formulae. Depending on species, points are awarded for antler length and thickness, length of tines, symmetry of antlers, weight, pearling and "beauty points". Negative scoring may apply. Marking will then lead to placement within a medal category - bronze, silver or gold, with points requirement differing between species. With practice, the stalker can learn to measure heads with reasonable accuracy, but any claim to official medal status will require submission of the head to an officially recognised examining body, such as the British Deer Society, the Game Conservancy or the St. Hubert Club of Great Britain. Certificates and/or medals may then be purchased from the same bodies. Alternative measurement systems are in use elsewhere, such the Douglas Score, developed in New Zealand by Norman Douglas, or the North American Boone & Crockett system; but these are seldom used in Ireland or Europe.

Evaluation is on the basis of a number of factors, including representative quality i.e. symmetry and balance, with no abnormalities, as well as on length of antlers and tines. Aspects of "beauty" may be subjective; they involve negative scoring points, and this is where the experience of the recognised examining bodies and individuals comes into play.

The following are the C.I.C. Medal Categories for the three Irish deer species:

Species	Bronze	Silver	Gold
Red deer	160.00-169.99	170.00-179.99	180.00 and over
Fallow deer	160.00-169.99	170.00-179.99	180.00 and over
Sika deer	225.00-239.99	240.00-254.99	255.00 and over

Note: criteria for Irish red deer are taken as for Scottish red deer. The point requirement for English red deer differs. Similarly, Irish sika are taken as Japanese sika; the requirement for Manchurian sika is higher. The differences for both variations are as follows:

Species	Bronze	Silver	Gold
English red deer	165.00-179.99	180.00-194.99	195.00 and over
Manchurian sika	300.00-349.99	350.00-399.99	400.00 and over

Measuring heads to the necessary degree of accuracy requires practice, especially if claim is being laid to medal status. All measurements are taken in metric, with those in centimetres taken to the nearest 0.1 cm and those in millimetres taken to the nearest 0.1 mm. Weights for red and fallow deer are taken in kilograms to the nearest 10 g. Only whole or half points are given under formulae which allow for beauty or malformation. To ensure accuracy, callipers should be used in conjunction with a fine metal tape measure and great care taken to establish where a tine begins and ends. The weight factor (required for red and fallow under C.I.C. rules) is taken on the basis of a long-nose cut (i.e. from the back of the skull, through the lower part of the eye cavity to a point immediately below the nasal bone), with deductions from 0 to 10 kg (0 to 10 points) depending on species, for weight included in full skull or other cuts. Fully mounted red and fallow deer cannot be measured under the C.I.C. formula because of this weight factor (unless the presenter is prepared to accept the maximum deduction). Beware of the possibility of hybridisation when evaluating sika deer heads. One possible guide is the length of the nasal bone; experience of hybridised Irish sika suggests that a nasal bone of length greater than 7.5 cm indicates a possible - indeed, a probable - red/sika hybrid.

TROPHY PREPARATION

Trophy heads, whether intended for submission for C.I.C. evaluation and measurement, or destined to hang on the wall as a personal reminder of the shot, may be full mounted (i.e. mounted with skin and eyes on a composition mould) or skull mounted. If the former, great care must be taken both in skinning the animal and in preserving the skin properly between skinning and tanning prior to mounting by a taxidermist.

The animal should be skinned as soon as possible after shooting, having taken care not to damage the hide by dragging over uneven or stony ground. Early-season skins are generally more subject to hair loss than mid or late season ones. A generous cut should be made well back from the neck, around the shoulders (as per diagram). Remember that the person eventually looking at the full-mounted head will view it from the front, and below, so the second cut should run vertically along the length of the nape, from shoulders to back of head, and a "Y" cut from the back of the head to the base of each antler. Peel the skin away from the neck all around before cutting off the head, which is done by finding the small junction of bones and sinews at the very top of the spine, where the head joins the neck. A small cut here, and then around the flesh of the upper neck and throat, and the head will come off with just a simple twist. At this stage, unless you are fully competent at skinning, it may be best to leave the job of skinning the head to the taxidermist, who will also be better able to judge the size of form on which to mount the head and antlers by seeing the original skull with skin on. Skinning the head with a view to full mounting requires care and skill not to damage the skin in removing it, but with practice becomes easier. A small very sharp knife is adequate, or better still, a scalpel.

The skin, on or off bone, should then be treated with a dry mixture, either of straight salt, or with some alum mixed in, having made sure that all remnants of meat, tissue and excess moisture have been removed. Properly salted, it will keep in ordinary conditions (not exposed to excessive heat, moisture or flies) for some weeks before further handling by the taxidermist; but not in a plastic bag, which encourages heat and early decomposition. Instead, store the skin and/or head in an ordinary hessian sack. If freezing for any period of time, roll up well and pack, this time in a plastic sack, to avoid freezer burn and skin damage. Don't store or freeze for longer than is necessary.

Heads not intended for full mounting may be skinned before boiling off flesh and tissue (the skin may be just as easily left on for boiling, but this makes for a messy solution to be disposed of after boiling). They may also be cut to the required format before boiling, as this will save time; although you may find it easier to achieve the desired cut after boiling and drying. The head or heads should be boiled, then allowed to simmer for two to three hours. Check the boiling water occasionally to make sure that heads do not over-boil, resulting in possible damage to the skull, especially break-up of the nose bone.

Having cleaned off all flesh and tissue, the head is then boiled a second time, this time with a mild solution of bleach added to the boiling water. Ordinary domestic bleach is quite suitable. Take care that only the bone of the skull, and not the antlers, touches the bleach solution.

After the second boiling, allow the skull to dry before applying an undiluted bleach to the bone, either painted on with a brush, or applied to cotton wool which is then wrapped carefully around the bone. This may be left on the skull overnight, or until the bleach has evaporated from the cotton wool. Once dried, the skull is ready for cutting and mounting.

SKULL CUTS

There are three standard skull cuts - skull top, short nose or long nose. The skull top cut is usually resorted to when over-zealous boiling has taken place, or the skull is otherwise damaged. Otherwise, either the short or long nose cut is equally acceptable. Antlers which are white, either because they have been accidentally bleached, or because they are early-season heads taken in velvet, can be stained by painting with a solution of permanganate of potash, which is purple in colour when put on wet but which dries to the correct shade of brown (which can be deepened if necessary, by applying another coat of the solution). The tips of the tines can then be whitened again by rubbing down with a fine sandpaper. A solution of turpentine and linseed oil (half and half) can be used to give the antlers a natural matt finish. To fix the head to a wooden shield, first fill the brain cavity with plastic wood, with or without a small piece of real wood set into the plastic filler, and insert the screw or screws from the back of the shield, into rawlplugs set into the plastic wood or wood plug. Do not set the screw in from the front as this spoils the appearance of the mounted antlers.

Choice of shield is up to the stalker. Any local wood-turner can make up shields from a standard pattern at minor cost, depending on choice of wood, while most jewellers' shops can provide a small engraved plate to set off the trophy.

APPENDIX VIII

PLANNING THE CULL: THE HOFFMAN PYRAMID, IN PRINCIPLE AND IN PRACTICE

It is an unfortunate fact that few stalkers in Ireland have the opportunity of managing wild deer on a long-term basis, other than on a handful of large estates or tracts of land where deer can be tolerated to an extent not possible in a pure timber-production environment and where broader objectives, beyond basic numbers control, can be pursued. The limitations of the present forest licensing system are such as to demand extreme focus on control of numbers, with the objective of reducing numbers to the minimum level commensurate with economic interests, without seeking to eliminate deer entirely.

In the broader deer management environment, the traditional approach has been vested in the Hoffman Pyramid, a method designed to provide an easy-top-understand visual presentation of deer population by age and sex and leading to a clear understanding of what deer (according to age and gender) should be culled. Established authorities including A. J. de Nahlik (Wild Deer – Culling, Conservation and Management, Ashford Press, 1987, Management of Deer and Their Habitat, Wilson Hunt, 1992) have long been proponents of the system, which lends itself to better deer management in circumstances of strict control.

The Hoffman Pyramid is built up over eight stages (but needing two years' observation and actual cull to set it up):

i)   Establish the average life span of deer in the locality ('A' = age)

ii) Establish the population of deer as appropriate to the ground ('P' = population)

iii) Draw a triangle on graph paper, with 'A' height, 'P' area and 'N', the number of deer, forming the base of the triangle.

iv) Calculate the number of calves born annually. Assume 50:50 birth ratio, males to females, with number born based on 100% of number of females forming right-hand base of your triangle. Now draw in a square representing each calf across the base of the triangle, males on left-hand side, females on right-hand side. This will create a 'wing' across the base of the triangle, widening the base on either side.

v)   Now decide your annual cull, based on the cull objective e.g. maintenance or reduction of population, manipulation of gender balance, enhancement of 'trophy' potential. This will alter the shape of the triangle, to a trapezoid (a trapezoid is a quadrilateral with exactly two parallel sides, which may be of unequal length).

vi) Convert the straight-line bisects of the trapezoid into yearly steps. This will show you how many deer of each age you should have – which in turn depends on the cull objective.

vii) Divide the pyramid population into four groups on either side of the 'age' line – giving you four cohorts on either side (calves at base, young or immature, mature and 'old', males on the left, females on the right). This fifth stage effectively becomes the starting point for continuing use of the pyramid model in succeeding years. Copy and shade or colour the triangle you have just created and overlay it on the previous year's version, but lower down i.e. allowing for one year's population growth.

viii) The unshaded squares represent your cull for the year under consideration. If the pyramid is the first available (i.e. if no previous records, on which to build a comparative version, exists), then simply assume a 100% calving rate for all females other than female calves and build cull squares above the line accordingly. The pyramid can be manipulated to provide cull targets which will lead to an overall reduction in population while maintaining the ideal 1:1 male:female ratio, by simply moving the (first) shaded pyramid from right to left or from left to right, depending on which gender needs to be culled more radically.

(This synopsis of the Hoffman Pyramid construction process is drawn from de Nahlik, A. J. [1992], Management of Deer and Their Habitat, Principles and Methods, at p. 117 *et seq.*, to which readers are directed for further information. See also Wild Deer – Culling, Conservation and Management, [1987] by the same author, at p. 28 *et seq.*).

APPENDIX IX

LARDER RECORDS

Although there is no legal requirement to maintain detailed larder records relating to deer killed (whether sold or not) hunters intending to dispose of surplus carcases by sale to a licenced Wildlife Dealer are advised to maintain adequate records of deer culled, in the form of a detailed Larder Record. The following information should be recorded:

- Species
- Sex
- Age, (if age determination is important to the management objectives, lower jaws should be stored for an independent check at a later date)
- Date (relates to body condition and reproductive status)
- Details of where shot (location)
- Bullet damage (relates to carcass value)
- Carcass contamination (relates to carcass value)
- Embryo presence/absence (relates to reproductive status)
- Udder presence/absence of milk (relates to reproductive status)
- Hill weight — gralloched with head, legs and pluck attached
- Nett Larder Weight — gralloched with head, legs and pluck removed, measured in metric, and the weight at which price/kg is given by the dealer. Note: head and pluck must not be removed if sold to a game dealer.

Health, disease and meat quality

- Behaviour before shooting, if out of the ordinary
- Abnormal organs: mouth, tongue, lungs, bladder, kidneys
- Peritonitis or adhesions between viscera and abdominal wall
- Condition of lymph nodes

WILDLIFE DEALER RECORDS

Wildlife Dealers are required to record the following details in the form of a Game Purchase Report/Receipt (and to issue the hunter supplying the carcase with a copy of the form on which the details are recorded):

- Name of Wildlife Dealer
- His VAT number
- His CRO registration number, if a company
- His EU approval number
- Supplier name (name of hunter)
- Deer Hunting Licence number
- Delivery date
- Delivery time
- Species
- Sex
- Date shot
- Time shot
- Dealer's tag number
- County is which shot
- Location at which shot

APPENDIX X

BALLISTICS

Calibre	Bullet Weight	Velocity (ft/sec)			Energy (ft/lbs)			Bullet Drop (inches, 'scope set @ 100 yds.)			
	(grains)	Muzzle	100 yards	200 yards	Muzzle	100 yards	200 yards	150 yds	200 yds	250 yds	MRD*
.22/250	55	3707	3192	2741	1616	1198	883	-0.5	-1.9	-5.0	
5.6 x 57 m.m.	74	3410	3050	2700	1910	1530	1195	-0.5	-1.9	-4.0	230
.243	100	3070	2810	2560	2100	1755	1460	-0.6	-2.4	-5.6	215
6.5 x 57 m.m.	93	3310	2920	2560	2260	1760	1355	-0.6	-2.4	-4.9	215
6.5 x 54 M. Sc.	159	2200	1940	1710	1710	1330	1030	-2.7	-7.8	-14.8	145
6.5 x 68R	127	3050	2805	2575	2615	2210	1865	- 0.6	-2.5	-5.0	215
.270 Win.	130	3170	2840	2560	2900	2325	1890	-0.7	-2.4	-5.2	215
.270 Win.	150	2935	2670	2410	2865	2365	1925	-0.8	-3.0	-6.6	205
7 x 57	123	2955	2625	2190	2390	1890	1485	-0.9	-3.1	-7.0	195
7 x 64	162	2890	2630	2390	3000	2485	2055	-0.1	-3.1	-6.6	200
7 m.m. RM	162	3150	2885	2625	3570	3000	2480	-0.5	-2.3	-5.1	220
.308 Win.	150	2855	2545	2255	2710	2150	1690	-0.9	-3.4	-7.6	190
.30-06	150	2990	2660	2505	2220	2970	2350	-0.7	-3.0	-6.6	195
.300 Win.Mag.	165	3180	2880	2600	3710	3045	2480	-0.5	-2.2	-5.2	220

Note: There are numerous other calibres available and a multitude of bullet weights and types available in each calibre. Those shown are standard factory loads, in some cases recommended for thick-skinned game up to and including red deer, in others, not. Inclusion or exclusion in this table should not be interpreted as a recommendation for or against use.

Source RWS/Dynamit Nobel.

*MRD = Manufacturer's "Most Recommended Distance" (yards)

APPENDIX XI

OTHER EUROPEAN DEER SPECIES

With a requirement for hunting tests operative in many other Member States of the European Union, it is hoped that in time, a reciprocal arrangement will be in place for the mutual recognition of qualifying tests of hunter competence. While most of the basics regarding firearms, safety, field craft and stalking techniques will be the same regardless of jurisdiction, some mention should be made of the species which may be encountered by the Irish hunter stalking abroad, including species not found in Ireland.

RED DEER

Distribution is widespread across Europe. In Britain, the main population is found in Scotland, both in the Highlands and in South West Scotland. The main centres of population in England are the West Country (SW England), Cumbria and Norfolk. On continental Europe the species is found in most countries from France across to the new EU accession states in eastern Europe. In general, the body size and antler quality increases moving west to east across Europe. Red deer are also found on the west coast of Norway and in southern Sweden. There are isolated populations to be found in Spain, Italy and the Balkans. The general biology of British and European red deer is as for Ireland.

FALLOW DEER

Fallow deer are widespread across continental Europe, and in Britain, in much of Scotland (excluding most of the Highlands and the central belt), throughout England and in much of North Wales. They are found also in southern Sweden and in all of the northern European countries. They are absent from most of the countries surrounding the Adriatic with the exception of a population on the western coast of Italy. Fallow deer are found on Sardinia but not Corsica. There is also a population in western Spain and in southern Portugal.

SIKA DEER

As in Ireland, most populations of sika deer in other European countries have originated from escapees from park collections, dating back to the early part of the 20th century. They are widespread now in the north of Scotland where hybridisation with red deer has also occurred. They are also found in isolated populations in southern Scotland, Cumbria, Hampshire and Dorset. Further afield, isolated pockets of sika deer are found in Denmark, Germany, France and Poland.

ROE DEER

Roe deer are found in every country of Europe with the singular exception of Ireland, although the area around Lissadell in Co. Sligo was home to a thriving population in the period to about 1930, when they were deliberately shot out prior to the planting of forests there under Ireland's infant forestry programme. Roe are a small deer with a reddish brown coat in summer, moulting to grey-brown in winter. Uniquely for European deer, the roebuck casts its antlers in November and grows a new set over the winter months. In April of each year the mature bucks will have shed their velvet and they then begin to establish territories which they will hold until antlers are cast again the following November.

The roe deer rut is from mid July to mid August. When mated, the doe undergoes a form of delayed implantation of the embryo into the wall of the uterus, which causes the fawn, or kid as it is sometimes called, to be born the following May or June, at the same time as the young of other deer species. This allows the dam the benefit of better feeding and the fawn more available cover and warmer weather. In areas of good feeding many roe does will carry twins. Triplets are not uncommon. Roe deer can do considerable damage to young forests and twinning allows for rapid increase in the population if efficient and consistent management is not practised.

Roe deer (buck)

Roe deer (doe)

MUNTJAC

Muntjac are a small dark brown deer originating in eastern China but released in the wild in a number of locations in England, where they have colonised most of the southern counties. In recent years they have been introduced in Belgium and the Netherlands. There have been a small number of sightings in Ireland (Wicklow and Wexford) in recent years but are not yet believed to be established here. Muntjac can be quite territorial. The bucks have small antlers and long upper canine teeth which are used in combat with other bucks. The female muntjac has no defined breeding season. Females come into season at seven months of age and gestation is seven months. The doe will come into heat immediately after fawning and therefore is pregnant on a virtually constant cycle. This lack of seasonality in breeding, together with their size and reproductive rate makes population control difficult. The usual practice is to cull all females that look pregnant, as they are themselves unlikely to have a dependent fawn.

Muntjac (buck and doe)

CHINESE WATER DEER

Chinese water deer are localised in two areas of southern England, farmland around Woburn and Whipsnade in Bedfordshire, near deer parks from which they originally escaped, and in the fens and broads of East Anglia to which they were introduced and which is very similar to their natural habitat. As their name suggests, they are native to China. Male Chinese water deer have no antlers but have long canine teeth which they use to settle disputes. They are sandy brown in colour, with a thick winter coat. The population has in the past been controlled mainly by hard winters but they have thrived in more recent milder weather and warmer winters. Their rut is in November – December, when the buck can be heard to make a whistling call. Like muntjac, which are found in similar country, they will bark when alarmed. Fawns are born in May – June like most other deer species, but unusually for deer, there can be a litter size of up to six young born.

Chinese Water Deer

European Elk

ELK OR MOOSE

The elk, as it is called in continental Europe, is the same species as that called moose in North America. It is the largest European deer species and is found in Norway, Sweden, Finland, Poland, the Baltic States and into Russia. They have a dark brown coat in both summer and winter, with a shoulder height of over two metres. They have a prominent bulbous nose which allows them to feed on water plants in lakes by closing their nostrils. Antler size in Europe is less than in North America, with only relatively small palmation evident even in mature bulls. They are not especially gregarious, usually being seen singly. The cow usually has twin calves, born without spots. The rut usually takes place in September.

REINDEER

Wild reindeer are found in the mountainous areas of southern Norway and in the arctic area of eastern Finland. They should not be confused with the semi-domesticated forms found in the Lapland area of Scandinavia. Both males and females have antlers, although those of the female are much smaller than those of the male. They have proportionately large feet, an asset in snow, which they have to scrape away to get at the lichen on which they feed during the winter months. Single calves are born in June and they soon join the main herd of females. The males remain solitary for much of the year.

Reindeer (adult male)

WHITE-TAILED DEER

The American White-tailed deer was introduced to south-western Finland where they have done well in the native conifer woodland of that region. In size and conformation they look very similar to fallow deer but in fact are more closely related to roe deer. They are reddish brown in summer, with a grey coat in winter. They have a wide tail, which is held erect when alarmed. The white hairs under the tail and around the rump patch give this species its name. Unlike Irish deer species, the white-tailed buck has an antler main beam which slopes backwards and then forward again in an arc, with the tines (other than the brow tine) facing backward.

White-tailed deer (doe & calf)

White-tailed deer (buck)

APPENDIX XII

OUTLINE OF RANGE TEST:
FORMAT FOR HCAP SHOOTING COMPETENCE TEST

Candidates for assessment under the Hunter Competence Assessment Programme must satisfy accredited examiners in the written multi-choice examination before proceeding to the shooting competence test. Criteria for management of the test are as follows:

PART 1: SHOOTING COMPETENCE

- The test is to be conducted only on an approved and insured rifle range.

- No zeroing of rifles will be permitted on test days. The onus is on the candidate to have an accurate rifle, just as it would be on a day's deer stalking.

- The initial part of the test is **three shots** to be placed in a **four-inch circle** at a distance of 100 metres. The candidate must lie prone for this.

- Should the candidate complete the test satisfactorily, he will be then allowed to proceed to the second test. Should the candidate fail this, one second chance is allowed. Failure a second time will mean the candidate will have to repeat the test on another day.

- The second part of the test requires the candidate to fire **six shots** at a deer shaped target. Each shot must be within the **seven-score ring** on the target.

      2 shots prone or sitting at **100 metres**
      2 shots sitting or kneeling at **60 metres**
      2 shots standing at **40 metres**

- All normal stalking aids are allowed in this test e.g. sticks, rucksack or bipod.

- All six shots must be fired before scoring.

- A candidate who fails this test is only allowed to repeat the test if he did not require a second attempt at the first test. In such a case, failure a second time will mean the candidate will have to repeat the test on another day.

- In both tests a bullet hole touching a line is classed as "in".

- The chief examiner's decision will be final.

PART 2: ORAL EXAMINATION ON SAFETY ISSUES

Each candidate will be examined orally on issues affecting safe firearms handling and firearms safety in the field.

The candidate is expected to respond satisfactorily to ten questions selected at random from a bank of approximately twenty-five questions. "Satisfactory response" is defined as a full and adequate demonstration of knowledge of ordinary requirements affecting safety, in the context of practical firearms handling.

Candidate response will be assessed by two assessors appointed for the purpose by the Assessment Committee.

APPENDIX XIII

THE COUNTRY CODE

- Guard against all risk of fire, especially in forest areas. Do not light any fires and please ensure that all matches are well extinguished before dropping them.

- Fasten all gates - they are there to control stock movements. Escaped animals can damage crops or come into danger on roads - or they can become mixed with other animals and difficult to separate again.

- Keep your dog under close control, especially near stock. Worried animals can become sick or go into shock. Pregnant animals can miscarry. Young animals can be attacked and even killed.

- Keep to public paths across farmland. Please never trample on crops. Remember they are someone's livelihood. If you leave a path, it can be difficult to find the next gate or stile and - especially on the hills - it can be quite easy to get lost in a very short space of time.

- Always use gates and stiles to cross fences, hedges and walls. Please do not attempt to climb over fences or walls. They are easy to damage and costly and time consuming to repair.

- Leave livestock, crops and machinery alone. Both animals and farm machinery can be very dangerous to touch. Never touch farm chemicals or animal foodstuffs.

- Please take your litter home - it is dangerous for animals (who may attempt to eat food remains or bags, or cut themselves on glass or hard plastic) and unsightly for local people and other users.

- Help to keep all water clean. Do not empty any liquids into rivers, watercourses or troughs.

- Protect wildlife, plants and trees. Do not pick wildflowers and never, ever remove a whole plant or bulb. Be careful near young trees whose trunks may be quite delicate.

- Take special care when driving on country roads. Farm vehicles can be very large and can travel very slowly. Animal herds may also be moving along roads and can be difficult to see until the last moment.

- Make no unnecessary noise. Radios and cassette decks are not welcome anywhere in the open countryside.